NEW DIMENSIONS OF WORLD POLITICS

NEW DIMENSIONS OF WORLD POLITICS

EDITED BY GEOFFREY L. GOODWIN and
ANDREW LINKLATER

A HALSTED PRESS BOOK

JOHN WILEY AND SONS
New York   Toronto

© 1975 Centre for International Studies

Published in the U.S.A., Canada and Latin America
by Halsted Press, a Division of John Wiley & Sons, Inc.,
New York.

Library of Congress Cataloging in Publication Data

Main entry under title:
New Dimensions of World Politics.

"A Halsted Press book."
Lectures given at the London School of Economics
and Political Science under the auspices of the School's
Centre for International Studies.
Bibliography: p.
Includes index.
1. International relations—Research—Addresses,
essays, lectures. I. Goodwin, Geoffrey L., ed.
II. Linklater, Andrew, ed. III. London School of
Economics and Political Science. Centre for
International Studies.
JX1291.N48   327'.07'2   74-32333
ISBN 0-470-31510-5

Printed in Great Britain

CONTENTS

PREFACE

The visits to London in the Spring and Summer 1974 of six distinguished American scholars provided the occasion for the public lectures now made more widely available in this book. The lectures were given at the London School of Economics and Political Science under the auspices of the School's Centre for International Studies. They are reprinted here very much in the form in which they were given, subject only to stylistic and other minor amendment. Each lecture was followed by a seminar discussion and the Introduction is based upon the record of these discussions kept by Mr Andrew Linklater.

The Centre for International Studies wishes to express its gratitude to the lecturers both for allowing their talks to be published and for agreeing that any royalties from this book should accrue to the Centre.

Geoffrey L. Goodwin   October 1974
Andrew Linklater

INTRODUCTION: CHANGING CONCEPTS OF STRUCTURE AND ORDER

Geoffrey Goodwin and Andrew Linklater

Traditionally, world politics has provided the stage on which the soldier and diplomat have taken the lead, their roles dictated by the interests of their political masters. Bankers, industrialists, scientists, even missionaries have lurked in the wings but have only rarely had more than walk-on parts. All this is changing, if the contributors to this book are to be believed.

In the first place, scientific and technological developments have helped to create new interdependencies among states, while the content of 'high politics' has expanded from the security realm to include not merely monetary, trade and aid matters but also the management and conservation of natural resources. In the second place, the world stage is now far more crowded, not only with more state actors but also with powerful multinational corporations and other transnational actors often vying successfully for the lead. The traditional perspectives of the soldier and diplomat with their preoccupation with the configurations of power no longer suffice. If we are to understand some of the most fundamental sources of change in contemporary world politics, and learn how to respond to them, we need to widen our perspectives and to have recourse to frames of reference beyond the actions of states.

Criticisms of the 'state-centric' approach are, of course, not new. In these papers, however, the criticism is given a new emphasis.'Vast, impersonal forces', which are not due to the deliberate contrivances of states, are said to be causing profound changes in the very structure of world politics. While the 'billiard ball' models offer useful categories for inquiry into the action and reaction of nation-states, they are held to be ill-equipped to promote the identification and understanding of these

1

subterranean forces. As a beginning the student of international relations must break out of existing 'conceptual jails' while the practioner readjusts the priorities of his national and milieu goals in the light of developments in world politics.

The term 'world politics' is to be preferred to 'international politics' or 'interstate' relations as an indication both of the changes afoot in the contemporary world and of the broader perspectives required for their understanding. Thus the term highlights the more pronounced changes within the structure of international society; it stresses the increasing interdependence of the members of that society; and it draws attention to the interpenetration of domestic and international politics. In these papers, therefore, two levels of analysis are employed. The first level corresponds to the question — 'what are the main characteristics of world politics?' The second level goes beyond description by asking — 'what are their longer term implications for the achievement of world order?' Implicit in both levels is the further question of how far traditional modes of analysis may need to be supplemented by new theoretical approaches to help illuminate the problems of structure and order in world politics.

Joseph Nye's contribution contains a carefully drawn list of six central characteristics or ingredients of contemporary world politics which 'state-centric' approaches tend to overlook. They are: (i) a decline of the efficiency of military power in the realisation of policy outcomes; (ii) the revolution in communications and the development of crossnational identification and linkage among groups of a similar social type; (iii) increased governmental activity and responsibility for social and economic welfare which extends the agenda of foreign policy; (iv) the diversification of issues which are central to world politics; (v) a greater differentiation of the types of international acto corresponding to this diversity of 'issue areas'; and (vi) the replacement of the soldier and diplomat as the fundamental 'actors' in the management of world order. To appreciate the deeper significance of these changes Nye argues that our analytical frames of reference need to be expanded and to draw upon the techniques of comparative politics and political sociology. In particular he looks to integration theory, shorn of its regional and teleological bias, to illumine the broader transnational and transgovernmental paradigms.

The other papers are concerned also that we escape from the 'conceptual jails' into which theories of 'power politics' are said to have led us. Each paper, in its particular way, recommends the redrawing of our 'cognitive maps' in order to understand (i) the transnational and transgovernmental dimensions (Nye); (ii) various forms of economic interdependencies (Rosecrance); (iii) the interconnectedness of military structures responsible for global order-keeping (Modelski); (iv) possible interdependencies arising from scientific and technological developments (Haas); (v) the interaction of elite attitudes and preferences with international order (Russett); (vi) the impact of current antimilitarism in the West upon the evaluation of the role of war in the maintenance of international order (Claude).

The second level of analysis seeks to evaluate the impact of these developments upon the structure of world order. At this level, one of the crucial themes is the decline of the autonomy and 'unconditional viability' of the nation-state. This is signified by the diminished immunity from events beyond the national frontier. Another source of decline of autonomy is the susceptibility to new forms of domestic constraint which render the state less capable of acting as a coherent unit. The costs of pursuing certain foreign policies have to include consideration of the tolerance of consumer-oriented and currently antimilitaristic populations. Mutual agreements between bureaucratic sectors of different states add elements of incoherence and indeterminacy into the policy-making process.

Moreover, to the extent that world order is more than the management of military power and the manipulation of interstate relations, the greater the need to investigate new kinds of interdependence as a basis of international order. What, it is asked, are the implications of new relations of interdependence for the maintenance of world order? What are the types of 'power structure' which can most readily exploit these linkage relationships and guide them in the direction of world order? How might present structures be reformed to conduce to new orders appropriate to a fluid and multi-dimensional international society? What are the considerations capable of leading elites to think in terms of structurally different bases of order?

3

All of the authors thus agree that fundamental changes are afoot in world politics and that we need to broaden our ideas of what should be included within the study of international relations to appreciate their possible implications. Yet it might be objected that the move from the first level, which sought to identify contemporary sources of change, to the second level, which raises questions about how to manipulate them in the service of order, begs a number of important questions. How far do these developments, collectively called 'world politics', constitute merely one sector in international politics? Are there not grounds for continuing to think that the central issues of international politics are those which affect the security interests of the great powers? Despite the increased importance of these new dimensions of world politics are there not compelling reasons for continuing to conceive of world order in traditional 'state-centric' terms? Certainly, the first four papers display a tendency to de-emphasise what can still be said in defence of 'state-centric' realism as a simple explanatory device. As an analytical tool rather than as a working model it continues to impose some order and structure upon the complex world one is attempting to understand. In addition, there is in these papers little sympathy for the view that politics is an art rather than a science and an underestimation of the extent to which political 'will' plays a part in shaping interstate relations.

It could also be contended that interdependence is a theme of Western politics and less typical of different regions or of the world at large. For nearly three decades the 'West' has formed something like a 'security community' in which, despite often acute differences of approach and emphasis, the threat of internal war has been (Greece and Turkey apart) a very remote possibility. This has hardly been the case for the world at large. There is also some plausibility in the view that societies with a Western kind of socioeconomic base are more likely to become involved in relationships which diminish the distinction between domestic and international politics. Societies with a prior commitment to 'capitalist development', scientific rationality, pragmatism and liberal-individualism may be more prone to interdependent relationships and less capable of acting as coherent units. This then raises the question of how far interdependence is in possession of its own momentum which will eventually entangle all societies? May it not be a condition to which states respond not so much because they exist in a highly competitive and decentralised environment but because they are committed to the kinds of values mentioned above? If so, why should it be supposed that it is then likely to become global in scope and that it is to these patterns of relationships that one should look in order to explore alternative structures for world order?

It would be parochial to ignore the importance of the arguments in these papers because of these uncertainties. The focus is after all upon the less tangible forces in world politics. The authors are concerned with the question of how elites should respond to interdependence where it is a fact, and where it may become a fact as states seek to establish new linkages with each other. The papers are far from asserting that the forces making for interdependence provide states with an automatic safe passage into untroubled waters. There is optimism in these papers but not of the kind which characterised much of liberal rationalist thought of the nineteenth and early twentieth centuries. Rosecrance agrees with Nye that interdependence is a highly ambivalent condition. Nye mentions the 'malign effects' of interdependence and Rosecrance its 'negative meaning'; interdependence can foster cooperation but it can also endanger international order by tempting states to pursue exclusive self-interested goals. The international economic system is currently delicately balanced between recognition of the need for new instruments of collective management to meet the pressures of interdependence and the very real possibility of states reverting to the 'beggar my neighbour' policies of the 1930s. Yet these authors maintain that elites could overcome the 'negative' tendencies of interdependence by adopting a more sensitive attitude to the creative possibilities which it has produced. By taking a longer term view, elites would perceive the possibility of using 'trade offs' between the issue-areas which entwine their societies as a basis for the enhancement of cooperation and the establishment of order. To enable this to happen, elites would have to readjust their priorities so that these forces of interdependence are regarded not as threats to national autonomy but as levers to be utilised to bring about large-scale change.

The remarks made in the first four papers concerning alternative structures of world order are among the most challenging. They are all concerned with how international interdependence can be made to work in a manner conducive to world order. Their common ground is the attempt to discover methods of constraining the power of the state to act alone and of encouraging it to identify its interests with those of other societies. Interconnectedness would frustrate the attempt to maximise one's interest through unilateral action by compelling the state to take into account the aims of other societies. Nye gives examples of transnational and transgovernmental relations and indicates how state autonomy is eroded by articulating the interests of subgroups from other societies. Professors Rosecrance, Haas and Modelski consider structural impediments which constrain the self-oriented action of the separate national-state. Each of them looks to structures which transcend state boundaries as the possible key to the promotion of global order.

Rosecrance approaches this theme by considering possibilities for collective action inherent in the increasing interpenetration of domestic economies. Capital investment, currency deposits and trade are major economic realms whereby one state obtains a stake in the economy of another. Economic interdependence produces new 'adversary partner' relationships; i.e. in one dimension relationships between states display their mutual interests in each other's welfare and the positive incentives to mutual cooperation, in another the ingredients of potential conflict and competition are evident in policies of *'sauve qui peut'*. Moreover, since economic issues are increasingly politicised and national economies more vulnerable to movements of 'hot' capital, currency fluctuations, changes in the terms of trade and the deliberate manipulation of economic weapons for political ends, there is a heightened sensitivity to the unpredictable and uncontrolled implications of interdependence.

Thus intensification of friction is a clear possibility if states set dangerous precedents by opting for nationally-oriented solutions and competitively based policies. On the other hand, there are high political stakes in the maintenance of a minimal commitment to order and positive incentives to building upon existing partnerships. Rosecrance suggests that the basis of international economic order lies not so much in common allegiance and subordination to a system of standards and rules as in the manipulation of economic linkages and structural interdependencies. 'Adversary-partner' relationships need to be manipulated so that cooperation prevails over disintegrative tendencies.

In pursuit of the most efficacious techniques, Rosecrance draws heavily upon an analogy with order-keeping in interstate relations, namely the deterrent function of holding populations hostage under the threat of nuclear devastation. The originality of Rosecrance's thesis is that one can threaten to wield economic power so as to damage another state's economy not merely as a national weapon but in order to elicit cooperation and to dissuade that state from 'antagonistic' behaviour. The advantage of economic deterrence over the nuclear prototype is that it need neither be a policy of the last resort nor a trigger of mutual destruction.

What is the reasoning behind this approach? In a potentially disintegrative situation there is a need to create definite costs for deliberately uncooperative acts. The question is not 'is cooperation necessary?' but 'how can a required level of cooperation be made attractive and irreversible?' In a situation of little cooperation and minimal control states are tempted to act alone to safeguard themselves from the 'malign effects' of interdependence. If there is an absence of sanctions for noncompliance there is no guarantee that cooperation will be forthcoming. The question 'how can interdependence be manipulated to produce beneficial results?' has to be answered in terms of the kinds of sanction capable of securing cooperation. For Rosecrance cooperation must be 'enforced' by building into the structure positive benefits of cooperation and prohibitive costs for noncooperation. Order and cooperation depend upon the deterrent power that can be brought to bear upon a dissenter. The self-interested state aware of the need to choose between its self-oriented goals and mutual cooperation must be induced to cooperate because of the deprivation threatened by its adversary-partners.

What are the difficulties with this approach? In the first place, it lacks generality. The interdependence of domestic economies is not a global phenomenon. It is still mainly a characteristic of the industrial market economies. Nevertheless, as states form new linkages between economic and political and security issues adversary-partner relationships may become more typical and the scope for this kind of deterrence could become considerable. The possibility of 'trade offs' between different issue areas has also already been demonstrated (e.g. American wheat sales to the Soviet Union in return for exit visas for Soviet Jews) and may well be increased.

A second objection, which is raised in Rosecrance's paper, is that the threat of war can produce configurations of power which endanger the existence of the whole system. Similarly, the threat to one's economic hostages is not separable from the possibility that widespread retaliation will result causing equally detrimental results. It might be argued that the risks contained in economic deterrence are a function of continuing to think in terms drawn from 'power politics'. If the focus is upon the longer term implications of change in world politics, should one still cling to a frame of reference so evidently based upon 'state centric realist' assumptions?

An investigation of the kinds of structure which can be superimposed upon adversary-partner relations is crucial for the understanding of interdependence and world order. In the light of the current oil crisis it is also of considerable contemporary significance. Rosecrance discusses the oil crisis as a litmus paper test of the future of interdependence in the West. The strong temptation to secure bilateral deals with the oil producers could create adversary relations within the West as each state sought to earn a surplus at the expense of the others. Rosecrance discusses various types of collective approach available to the West and possible interdependencies between the West and the Arab oil producers. To offset the $40 - 60 billion annual additional oil import bill of the industrial market economies the oil producers might be induced to increase their holdings in sterling and dollars and Eurocurrency deposits, to invest in Western industries, to increase their own imports of industrial goods and to step up aid to less developed countries, especially those most hard hit by increased oil prices. To some degree all these measures are already in train, but the limits, especially of the latter two, are soon reached. The desirability of collective agreement between the industrialised West is evident enough, but what form should it take? A modest scheme for sharing oil during an energy crisis has been agreed — on paper, while on Mr Dennis Healey's (British Chancellor of the Exchequer) initiative the International Monetary Fund is to examine the possibility of augmenting its present special 'oil facility' recycling Arab oil earnings (i.e. the IMF borrows from oil producers and others to lend to member states) from the present $3 - 4 billion up to as much as $30 billion. It cannot be said, however, that the auguries for such a scheme are promising. Meanwhile the urgency of the situation does not diminish. Oil bills mount and will have to be met against a background of soaring inflation and economic recession and the political risks of intervention do not altogether rule this possibility out. In the longer run the cohesion of the West is in the interest of each, but is the necessary political will there?

At first sight, Modelski's essay emphasises the continuities rather than the changes in the international system. At least at the global level, the concentration of military power continues to be the central basis of order-keeping. The dominant structure remains bipolar although a slight deconcentration of power has taken place. The paper maintains that order is a function of a structure of relationships between the 'producers' of order and their 'clients'. This structure consists not of nation-states as such or of global economic regulatory services but of the military, political and diplomatic organisations which regularly act and interact on the global scene. To explain this structure Modelski invokes concepts derived from the study of oligopolistic industries. Order is the function of the relationships between the structures of adversary-partners. To preserve their dominant position these structures collude to safeguard the *status quo*. The attempt to prevent the proliferation of nuclear weapons is the kind of arrangement which adversary-partners wish to secure and to extend into other areas of mutual interest.

Modelski calls for closer enquiry into the implications of different power structures for order and stability. What, for example, are the respective merits and demerits of a bipolar and multipolar system? Both systems are described as types of oligopolistic structure 'characterised by the interaction of a very few but complex and powerful actors' capable of exerting an immediate impact upon all the others. From the public point of view, Modelski holds that there is little substantial difference between these two patterns of interdependence between adversary-partners. Each system is 'capable of producing relative periods

9

of stability', but each is wasteful of resources and conflict prone. Neither has much to commend it.

Consequently, Modelski considers the free market as a vantage point from which to evaluate alternative structures of interdependence. Since no significant deconcentration of power has taken place one must think in terms of the deliberate creation of alternative structures. Freedom of movement and information, the dispersal of technological expertise and the deliberate deconcentration of power would characterise the free system. Additionally, the strengthening of international peacekeeping action would displace the activities of the major powers. From Modelski's viewpoint, alternative structures should also be judged in terms not only of what is the rational distribution of functions between already existing and alternative structures, but, more importantly, who is regarded as having the *right* to rule. In other words, the issue is as much one of the legitimacy of the rulers as of the military might they can muster. What are the preconditions and possibilities of such a deconcentrated system ever being accepted? What kinds of changes of elite perspectives would have to occur before general agreement upon the desirability of this kind of system and the norms implicit in it was forthcoming? Can we discern any forces in world politics which seem likely to generate change in this direction? A deeper understanding of some of the considerations to bear in mind while thinking of these questions can follow from a consideration of the issues raised by Professor Haas's contribution.

Haas investigates an alternative but ambiguous source of change in the contemporary world, namely the possible impact of science and technology upon the future international order. Attitudes towards scientific advances are ambiguous because they reflect both (i) the belief that science is a progressive and evolutionary force on account of its superior epistemology; and (ii) the disenchantment with science on account of the intractable social and political problems brought in its wake and the limitations of its methodology, and that of derived social science, to illumine the ends of social and political life. In other words, scientific knowledge is superior but flawed; it is good on means, but silent on ends.

The political impact of science and technology has hitherto been to strengthen the hand of the separate state. The anxieties caused by science could, however, become increasingly internationalised as the nation-state loses the capacity to handle the problems caused by applied science. To cope with oceanic and atmospheric pollution, food and energy requirements, population increase and so forth, the state will have to reconsider its status as the fundamental international actor. As too many crucial variables lie outside national control the nation-state will become outmoded in this sector and further internationalisation will become essential. Our anxieties about science could become a most powerful trigger of large-scale structural change in the international system. Haas reminds us that our understanding of the past is of little assistance in identifying the kinds of problems which could arise in the future. Furthermore, an imaginative leap will be required if political elites are to grasp the opportunities for reforming and creating institutions able to cope with these new developments. By discussing three scenarios of the future the paper indicates how we shall have to stretch and change our current images of institutional arrangements in order to reconcile the fruits of scientific research with social and political goals.

A discussion with Professor Haas on the 1974 Law of the Sea Conference attempted further to investigate some of the conditions of change in the international system. What did experience at the Conference tell us about the relationships between elite preferences and the likelihood of changes in the structure of international order? What kind of restraints upon their sovereignty might coastal states be ready to accept to secure a twelve-mile territorial sea or a two hundred-mile economic zone? What are the preconditions of the establishment of an International Seabed Regime and the application of the principle of the 'common heritage of mankind' to the use of the sea bed resources beyond national jurisdiction.

Professor Haas's argument depends heavily upon the assumption that the activity of politics will undergo substantial changes as elite perceptions become imbued with scientific orientations. Scientific advances would create similar constraining forces upon diverse elites; this would in time lead to a convergence of elite attitudes which would in turn facilitate the establishment of new structures. Haas maintains

11

that political elites will be unable to bend instrumental knowledge to their political will because this will is increasingly a function of scientific perspectives as applied to public policy.

Did behaviour at the Law of the Sea Conference suggest that these changes were becoming, however gradually, an integral part of diplomatic relations? On the contrary, from experience so far it could be argued that the heterogeneity of elites, their mutual suspicions and contrasting ends, their symbolic rather than merely instrumental attachments to the nation-state, would continue to be obstacles to the creation of new structures and institutional arrangements. The main impulse to structural change had been the fear of a break down of the conference — and the opportunities it might afford the strong. Yet no dominant link issue had concentrated elite attention on collective rather than national or subnational interests. Indeed, many domestic pressure groups had pressed for disaggregation of issues. There was, in fact, a need to trace the relative merits of aggregation (so as to produce possible 'trade offs') and the fractionating of issues. Although Haas remains optimistic that elite convergence will become a reality, he stresses that the perception of future crisis or violence is one of the necessary conditions of readiness to support alternative structural arrangements. Haas focuses upon three factors which will influence the willingness of elites to enter into new structural arrangements: environmental constraint, elite convergence and political 'will'. There is, however, a tendency to regard political 'will' as a product of the first two factors. How far does Haas overlook the probability that neither environmental constraint nor an increased scientific orientation will automatically produce a willingness to cooperate positively? Political elites may respond quite differently to environmental pressures and put science to very different uses.

Consequently, a greater understanding of elite perspectives and values would be a major contribution to the kinds of approach so far discussed. They have tended to focus upon structures and mechanisms through which states become constrained to cooperate in the maintenance of order. One of their shortcomings is that they neglect the role of values in the bases of order and the necessary adjustments of elite perspectives if alternative structures are to be promoted. Attempts to explore the role of elite attitudes in international order are more central to the discussions of Russett and Claude.

Russett agrees with Modelski on the formal point that the international environment has undergone less structural change than our attitudes and preferences have led us to believe. How is the static nature of the international system to be explained? As a test case Russett looks for contrasting explanations for the time-lag between the rise of disenchantment with and the opposition to the Vietnam war and the eventual withdrawal from it. Why was the interval as long as five or six years?

Russett analyses four putative explanations — the strategic, economic, ideological and bureaucratic. Each has a certain plausibility; each can to some extent be empirically tested. The difficulty is to assess their relative importance in any particular instance; and, one might add, to judge the status of whatever propositions one tentatively arrives at. To Russett traditional modes of enquiry are helpful but insufficient and he suggests the value of more intensive enquiries into elite performances. The paper attempts to do this with regard to the attitudes of defence industry executives. It gives an account of an as yet incomplete piece of research which sets out to test the hypothesis that these executives had an interest in promoting a pro-war ideology. At this stage of the research, the strongest indicators point to the conclusion that economic interests were less important than attitudes shared with other domestic groups. Business executives in common with other elite groups shared a deep concern for the effects of the war upon economic and social stability, and this was of prime importance in the formation of their attitudes.

The latter sections of the paper analyse some of the methodological difficulties involved in the study of elite attitudes. How does one discover how elites think and have thought? How does one contend with the selectivity of memory and the natural tendency of interviewees to present themselves in a good light? How can one be sure that their thoughts preceded action and are not retrospective evaluations of it? These are issues which more intensive research would hope to resolve.

Professor Claude's concern is with the problem of evaluating war. His paper assesses and evaluates the impact of the Vietnam war upon American, and indeed Western, conceptions of the place of war in the maintenance of international order. The principal effect has been widespread antimilitarism. In the spirit of Lippmann's and Kennan's conception of public opinion, Claude thinks that this could be due to a misconceived preoccupation with the immediate costs of war in terms of human suffering rather than the longer term benefits in terms of the achievement of political goals. The difficulty is that the former are painfully obvious, the latter elusive and controversial.

In the academic community the problem of war has taken on an exaggerated importance reflected in the development of peace research which approaches it in the spirit of a crusade against evil rather than as a problem to be understood. Claude argues for a return to the study of the structures of interstate relations which give rise to the incidence of war and of how we can prevent situations arising which can be held to necessitate and justify violence. The paper recommends a cost-benefit analysis of wars to identify and evaluate both the different segments of a war and the differing attitudes towards it on the part of the contestants. But one of the primary aims of this kind of analysis should be to assess the consequences of a particular war for the international system as a whole in terms of the changes in structure it has induced.

What is the overall significance of these papers? They should be of interest to proponents of widely contrasting approaches to the study of international politics. Their primary concern is the location of those forces which are creating change in the structure of world politics. They go beyond description of these forces (i) by suggesting that a broadening of traditional conceptual frameworks is a necessary condition for grasping their true significance; (ii) by claiming that an understanding of their significance should lead elites to readjust their policy priorities so as to exploit their growing interdependencies; and (iii) by posing a number of questions of a more traditional moral and political nature. In the remainder of this introduction a brief attempt will be made to assess the significance of these papers under these three headings.

(i) Most of the papers are critical of attempts to study international politics mainly from 'state-centric realist' assumptions. Two related comments can be made in reply. The first is that for the investigation of adversary relationships, and for the study of issues of power and security generally, 'state-centric' assumptions still provide a good starting point, if only because at this level states remain the main actors and each displays a certain unity of purpose and response. The second is that where partnership relations prevail, that is where a security community exists, more complex linkages between states are likely to be found; transnational and transgovernmental relations may then assume a much greater importance and their analysis may indeed benefit from a broadening of focus and from techniques borrowed from the study of, for instance, comparative politics and integration theory. The point is, however, that there are likely to be as many potentially rewarding approaches as there are relationships between the poles of 'amity' and 'enmity'. Methodological openmindedness is a precondition of appreciating the merits of the different emphases proffered by contrasting approaches. To which one might add that no single frame of reference could hope to produce a self-contained, fully explanatory theory for the understanding of the infinitely diverse patterns in international society.

(ii) The 'state-centric' model is criticised not only because of its one-sided implications for the understanding of world politics but also because it is held to blind the policy maker to the creative opportunities, immanent in new linkages and interdependencies, for the establishment of alternative structural and institutional arrangements.

Traditionally, the constraints upon policy makers which stem from the heterogeneity and quasi-anarchical condition of international society — and the need to retain domestic support — have been thought to provide compelling reasons for the priority both they and the academic community have given to the more immediate problems of security and welfare. It would not then be surprising if current international institutions were often neglectful of the longer term problems of international society. Yet this is merely to underline the value of academic inquiry into the long-term forces making for change. Such inquiry could at least help, through for example the trend projections proposed by Haas, to forestall situations where fundamental issues of world politics are set aside until only a crisis situation compels collective action. Policy makers might even be persuaded on occasions to reconsider their hierarchy of objectives so that longer term issues are not neglected but

15

become an integral part of policy agenda.

On the other hand, although new linkages and patterns of inter-dependence arising out of economic, scientific and technological pressures may produce new types of relationships, it is still not clear how much scope they are likely to offer elites for the establishment of structurally different forms of world order. May not one difficulty be that the totality of functional relationships is too complex, diverse and dispersed to allow elites to posit them as the bases of new structures? In which case might it not be more helpful to consider structural approaches to world order from a more traditional orientation? What are, for instance, the interdependencies which could conceivably transform adversary relations into adversary-partner relationships? What are the linkages which could transform the latter into relationships of a 'security community' dimension? Alternatively, what are the interdependencies which could lead to increased friction and adversary relationships? In this kind of analysis, the primary consideration would be 'which areas should elites attempt to link in order to add stability and reduce indeterminacy in their bilateral and multilateral relationships?'. To answer this question and to assess the implications for regional and global order, greater understanding of the operations of different patterns of interdependence is required.

(iii) The fact that interdependence could produce further internationalisation of issues and create incentives for collective action is a strong argument for assimilating questions of moral and political theory into our frame of reference. One of the recurrent themes of these papers is the need to adjust our cognitive maps in order to perceive sources of change in world politics. But more than this is needed. Not only must elite attitudes change if the possibilities for manipulating the forces making for interdependence are to be grasped, but they must face up to the normative questions that are bound to arise as national autonomy gives way to new forms of collective management, questions, for instance, about the kinds of international structure which ought to be established, about how to evaluate often competing national claims and interests in the context of the need for collective decisions, and above all about the most just way of distributing values.

Existing cognitive maps are ill-equipped for reasoning about questions

16

of this kind. There is little or no tradition of reasoning about the nature of international society comparable to reflections about the nature of the state. Moreover, by emphasising the subjective and emotive nature of human values, 'scientific' approaches have often hindered progress in this direction. To some extent this is reflected in the central orientation of the first four papers which is upon structural and mechanical pressures which will so constrain states that they are 'compelled' to follow cooperative policies. They look to forces which will create overwhelming incentives for rational and self-interested states to come to a joint articulation of objectives through collective action or new institutional arrangements. Every order depends upon the creation of positive incentives for cooperation and definite costs for antagonistic behaviour. The danger is that structural-mechanistic approaches of this kind can lead to an underestimation both of the role of common objects of identification and of the need for a commitment to a shared sense of justice and obligation in the maintenance of order.

In fairness, Modelski and Nye pay more attention to the normative dimension than either Haas or Rosecrance. They are more inclined to the view that the interaction of the structural and normative dimensions, albeit to different degrees, enter into the basis of all order. Yet it must still be asked whether some of the central presuppositions of their papers are not inimical to the parallel development of normative dimensions of inquiry.

A particular difficulty of Claude's paper is in fact the subordination of normative to systemic considerations. This paper recommends that an assessment of the costs and benefits of war upon the international system should be the prime concern of evaluation. Yet it does not seem to recognise that one of the characteristics of a major war is that it reflects a fundamental conflict of values within the international system. When a major war is indicative of the breakdown of the system, the system cannot be used as the criterion with which to evaluate the war. In this situation one cannot estimate the effects of the war upon one international system; one has to make a choice among the competing systems for which the contesting parties are struggling. To do this one has to possess moral criteria. Peace researchers may be apt to smuggle in moral preferences rather surreptitiously, but Claude, by emphasising the separation of personal values from research, has in his paper obscured the need to evolve moral criteria for choosing between different kinds of systems.

Haas and Rosecrance are sceptical of the desirability of the normative approach. They suggest that efficacy rather than the elaboration of superordinate goals is the fundamental problem of order. In Rosecrance's paper the paradigm assesses possible manipulation of interdependencies from an interesting position. It presupposes a concept of human rationality and motivation by which to evaluate the efficacy of new structures. By building positive incentives for cooperation and costs for antagonistic behaviour into the structure, cooperation becomes the most rational option for a self-interested state. The structure presupposes that states behave in accordance with a utilitarian self-interested calculus. If the policy of going it alone is made unprofitable states will comply with collective action. Undoubtedly, there are costs which virtually all societies wish to avoid, in comparison with which the costs of cooperation would be by far the lesser evil. Nevertheless, in less critical situations states often sharply disagree about both the levels of costs they are prepared to accept and the benefits which they deem necessary if they are to be induced to cooperate. This is, in itself, an obstacle to the operation of, for example, a structure of 'deterrence'. And since states make such different calculations of the value of cooperation the more obstreperous may hold out for the most advantageous 'offer' and so give rise to justifiable charges of injustice.

Without denying the importance of the criterion of efficacy, it is reasonable to object to a radical separation of the means and ends of political life. While the means must satisfy the idea of efficacy they ought not to be prejudicial to the development of an order based upon such notions as consent, justice and obligation. Indeed, the central theme of the first four papers is 'how can patterns of interdependence be manipulated to produce beneficial results?'. But beneficial by what criteria? The answer to this question partly depends on the needs and interests embodied in the conceptions of human good which are thought valuable and worth preserving. Consequently, if an alteration of our cognitive maps is essential to the understanding and management of changing patterns of interdependence then it must take into account these aspects of traditional moral and political theory.

It might be added that a theory which assumes that the way to induce states to cooperate is to appeal to their individual self-interest, cannot present a very convincing case for far-reaching international cooperation. From this perspective, all that can be said to a dissenting state which asks 'why should I cooperate?' is 'because it is in your interest'. The implication is that there is no justification of cooperation where a state is not convinced of the advantage to itself of cooperation. And, as we have seen, calculations of interest and advantage are apt to be focused on the short rather than the long-term. Yet these papers have suggested changes in our cognitive maps to meet the challenges of the 'world politics' of the future rather than the 'interstate relations' of the present; in effect the idea of an emerging world community is posited with the implication that its members will be under some kind of obligation to cooperate to the 'common good'. But we still need in the first place to think out what the 'good' might be, not only for ourselves but for societies other than our own. And in the second place we need to try to discern more clearly under what circumstances and in what dimensions of international life we can move from our present state in which the nuclear peril induces a sense of a shared predicament − 'man is a creature civilised by fear of death' − to a realisation of the extent to which our emerging interdependencies may foster a sense of mutual obligation on the basis of which we can approximate more closely to the 'common good'. These lectures, valuable as they are in other directions, have the virtue of focusing our minds on questions of this kind.

1 INTERNATIONAL INTERDEPENDENCE

Richard Rosecrance

' "You crossed my path on the fourth of January,' said Professor
Moriarty. 'On the 23rd you incommoded me; by the middle of
February I was seriously inconvenienced by you; at the end of March
I was absolutely hampered in my plans; and now, at the close of April,
I find myself placed in such a position through your continual
persecution that I am in positive danger of losing my liberty." ' (*The
Final Problem*)

Professor Moriarty knew that his and Holmes's fates were interdependent.
If Holmes triumphed, Moriarty would be destroyed. If Moriarty were
to succeed, Holmes had to be eliminated. And in the Conan Doyle
account the interdependence of these two men increases as their struggle
reaches its height. So it is with all adversaries. The greater the conflict of
interest between them, the greater their interdependence.

But this use of the term 'interdependence' is different from the usual
one. We have generally thought that 'interdependence' meant something
positive. *Inter*dependent nations were supposed to be more peaceable
than their *in*dependent counterparts. After the last war, many new
prophets of peace told us that the globe was effectively shrinking in size.
Revolutionary advances in transport and communications had brought
nations into much more closely knit patterns of intercourse. It was
almost as if mankind had been moved from a larger to a smaller space.
Jostling, bumptiousness, high spirits and pranks that might be perfectly
tolerable on a playing field or in a large but nearly empty enclosure
could not be tolerated in smaller quarters. Thus, it was asserted, nations
would have to 'behave'; to regulate their conduct very carefully in order
to avoid trampling upon one another. The dawning recognition that

mankind was interdependent in this latter sense was supposed to bring about international cooperation and peace.

Thus the term 'interdependence' has both positive and negative connotations. To depend upon one another may suggest the mutual self-support of close relatives or friends; the self-disciplined respect for the rights of others that one finds in the best classrooms; or alternatively the opposition of adversaries, whose destinies are inextricably intertwined.

To say that the world is interdependent, therefore, is really to say nothing about the amount of cooperation or conflict within it. The concept does suggest a kind of 'connectedness'. It does presume a strong relationship of interests. But it does not indicate whether that relationship is positive or negative.

The Development of Interdependence

An interdependent world did not develop quickly. Two or three hundred years ago states' interests were only partly interrelated. Owing to the rudimentary nature of communications and transportation one state's actions did not immediately and directly affect all other states. Militarily, wars were difficult and costly operations which could not be risked except on grounds of the most severe provocation. There were few really developed transnational links between nations. In the nineteenth century however this situation changed. As a result of new technologies of transport, communications and production, international trade and finance grew rapidly. By the latter part of the century shifts in the London bank rate came to have an enormous effect upon trading and financial operations in the rest of the world. A London-centred interdependent economic system emerged.

The interdependent economic system, however, did not prevent political and military conflict as World War I showed only too well. Nor did the closer intertwining of economic interests of Western states prevent the Great Depression. The world economic system collapsed under the assault of nationalistic economic policies. But the Depression had at least one beneficial effect: it caused governments to develop goals of full employment and social welfare for their citizens. It thus became necessary either for governments to try to insulate their populations from the impact of international economic trends, or, if this was impossible, to plan cooperatively for rising levels of world trade and domestic growth with which to sustain an approximation to full employment. From 1945 on, therefore, all economic occurrences would have political significance and the bases for political interdependence were established. A trend towards even greater interdependence emerged as economic forces carried world trade, investment and financial transactions to new heights.

The growth of the international economic sector since World War II has been unparalleled. Experts estimate that about one fourth of world GNP is now produced by corporations operating outside their home territories. The great multinational corporations have become so large that of the fifty largest economic entities in the world thirty seven are countries and thirteen are corporations. Of the top hundred, fifty one are corporations. Since 1945 the growth of the international sector has even outpaced that of the domestic. Ratios of foreign trade to GNP have greatly increased for most industrial countries.

States as political units are perhaps less in control of these trends than they once were. The enormous development of transnationalism — the growth of international transactions in which at least one of the parties is *not* a government — has made it more difficult for governments to influence or even to keep up with the pace of international economic change. The clearest example of transnationalism is, of course, the multinational corporation. But in a variety of economic, scientific and technological areas, international transactions among private units have grown so rapidly that they affect and even determine economic and financial decision making. In air transport, computers, nuclear energy, investment and the development of alternative energy sources, private decisions and technology lead and constrain public policy. Transnationalism is in one sense a beneficial phenomenon because its potency and scope are so large that governments may have to reach higher levels of cooperation and perhaps to institute new organisational forms of cooperation if it is to be effectively controlled. This requirement brings states closer together. In another sense, however, transnationalism is a negative development, because the necessary degree of governmental cooperation to cope with its problems may not be attained.

The new economic links among countries have come also to represent a different kind of stake in the international system. In 1913 most investment abroad was portfolio investment, largely consisting of bonds and other debt instruments rather than equities. Today an increasing proportion is direct investment involving not only ownership but also partial or complete control of productive facilities. This form of ownership is more difficult to transfer, and the capital it represents is less liquid than indirect investment. It therefore entails a proportionately greater and longer term commitment on the part of the foreign holder. Direct investment has grown greatly because it pays extremely well. To take but one case, in the United States foreign earnings on direct investment as a proportion of total domestic profits have risen from 9 per cent in 1950 to 28 per cent in 1969. Increasingly many nations have large and stable stakes in the economies of other states.

While these stakes have grown, the international economy has become somewhat less resilient and perhaps more fragile. International debts can be flexibly and easily discharged when all participants have large monetary reserves. Just as the game of poker becomes more tense as the stakes increase relative to individual holdings, so international financial dealings become worrisome when the amounts involved increase relative to national reserves. In 1945 total international reserves were 39 per cent greater than world exports. By 1971 total reserves were only 40 per cent of the value of exports. Fairly small shifts in trade could then lead to crisis measures by one or more states, perhaps causing a disruption in the rules of international commerce. The international economic system, therefore, is far more sensitive to the accumulation of surpluses and deficits than it used to be. Some even believe that this heightened sensitivity − the fact that one economy is much more quickly and drastically affected by changes in another than was the case, say forty years ago − is the truest measure of interdependence.

If national economies are even more directly and substantially affected by each other, there is a parallel development in political and military interdependence. It does not need to be said that the political and military impacts of national policy used to be rather small. Because of rudimentary technology, war took a long time to arrange; at least until World War I, there was a considerable scope for diplomatists and political leaders to arrange a solution before a test of arms occurred. Today the nuclear weapon means that certain forms of violence are in a state of perpetual mobilisation. The consequences of their employment would affect every living being on the earth's surface. Because of this the stakes involved in the preservation of a basically peaceful international order are exceedingly high. But it is still not certain that the degree of intergovernmental cooperation needed to prevent war in all circumstances will be attained. In economics as we have seen, transnational forces may upset relations among governments. In politics, actions by smaller states may disturb relations among the great powers. There is also potential for major power miscalculation.

The very high levels of political and economic interdependence which have been reached, therefore, by no means guarantee continuing cooperation among states. In politics, economics and finance a much more substantial apparatus of intergovernmental cooperation is required beyond levels which currently exist if peace and the contemporary world economy are to be preserved.

The Prospects for Cooperation

One must therefore examine afresh the prospects and possibilities for such cooperation. This question needs ultimately to be addressed in the current international context. But a brief detour through previous discussions of the possibility of cooperation in international relations may point us in the right direction. On the prospects of international cooperation there are two major strands of international relations theories: the one pessimistic; the other optimistic. The pessimistic view enunciated by Hobbes and also Rousseau notes that nations are in a state of nature, of perpetual '*warre*'. There is no superior legal, political, or military power to force them to cooperate. In international relations, moreover, the interest of the group or collectivity of nations and the interest of a particular state are not identical. However much importance a single state attaches to the preservation of the general peace, there will

24

always be occasions in which a specific act of war or noncooperation will benefit that state more than acceptance of a general regimen of agreement and peace. This conclusion is not the result of some failure of rational analysis; in the view of the pessimistic school it is rather commended by reason. In proof Rousseau offered the famous parable of the Stag and the Hare. In it a number of hunters in search of food are stalking a stag. The efforts of all of them are required if the stag is to be caught. During the chase, however, a hare runs across one hunter's path. This hunter faces the choice of stopping and catching the hare (thereby allowing the stag to escape) or continuing to pursue the stag. The rational choice for the single hunter, Rousseau argues, is to capture the hare even though this means that the others will not be able to attain their goal of catching the stag. His hunger will be easily satisfied by the hare, though the others will go hungry. Rousseau's argument rests upon the greater certainty of achieving the goal in the one case as opposed to the lesser certainty in the other. In this instance unless the hunter's agreement to help with the capture of the stag could be reliably enforced, he will surely act uncooperatively. So in international relations generally, states will often act against cooperative agreements and arrangements if it is in their direct and immediate interest to do so. Unfortunately, from the pessimistic point of view, binding and enforceable agreements do not exist. There is no legal enforcement power which operates without the consent of major states.

The pessimistic prediction of continual war and noncooperation among nations, however, has been challenged. Even Rousseau and Hobbes admitted that if an enforcement power existed, cooperation could be guaranteed. In the case of the parable, if the hunter who deserted his post to catch the hare could be punished for his antisocial behaviour, it is not likely that he would repeat the experiment. Thus the problem of attaining reliable cooperation in international relations depends upon the certainty of punishment for aggressive or antagonistic behaviour. Can such a certain sanction be promised? Even the optimists admit that in many, perhaps even most, international situations, the probability of punishment is very low. Thus, reliable deterrence of such action does not normally exist. Why is this so? First, it is because nations do not always see their vital interests affected by the uncooperative state's action. Second, it may be difficult or even impossible to try to punish the national transgressor. Punishment could have such severe consequences for the punisher, that he does not attempt it. It does not follow, however, the optimists point out, that deterrence is never successful. There are some acts which nations will fight to prevent. Nor is it always necessary to take suicidal risks to deter an aggressor. There are many steps in the escalation ladder between a sternly worded note and all-out war. The reconsolidation of alliances or alignments may also deter action through the traditional mechanism of the balance of power. Military demonstrations or expressions of resolve may be as effective as the actual use of weapons.

In certain ways, optimists point out, the ability to elicit cooperation through the threat of military action is higher today than in previous ages. In the nineteenth century a state had to fight to acquire hostages before it could sorely wound an opponent. An opponent's lines and fortifications had to be breached before his civilian population could be threatened. In the nuclear deterrence of the present day, however, both sides already hold the populations of other states hostage. One does not have to fight to acquire hostages. In this particular sense, threats are easier to make; the threat of punishment must therefore be taken more seriously by those who might be tempted to defy it.

Even the optimists admit, however, that deterrence also has crucial difficulties. If the threat is actually carried out, it has catastrophic consequences for all sides. Thus in most instances the threat of retaliation is simply not credible. Military deterrent instruments, moreover, are unbelievably crude. The hostages which nuclear states hold are opposing populations. These populations cannot be argued with; they cannot be persuaded; they cannot be influenced politically: they can only be killed. Thus the power over hostages is so massive and undifferentiated that it could only be used in the last resort. It certainly could not be employed to punish minor defectors from an international cooperative framework.

The increasingly interdependent world economic system, however, offers a new basis for regulating national conduct. The pessimists argued that states would not cooperate unless there were reliable penalties for noncooperation. Thus nations must have hostages — valued groups of people or property — which can be offered as guarantees of good behaviour. The international economic system produces a new kind of hostage and the basis for a different and possibly more successful form of deterrence. Among developed countries at least, the stakes which each nation has in the economic well-being of another have grown significantly. If a country sells a large proportion of its goods in one particular market (and trade among developed countries is becoming more concentrated geographically and in terms of specific commodities), that market is a kind of hostage. The host country's threat to that market can have a very reformatory effect. If a nation has a large share of direct investment in another country, that country is in a position to influence the profitability of investment by tax policy, economic policy, governmental regulation of competition and in numerous other ways. By increasing the stake which one country has in another, the impact of contemporary interdependence has been to provide hostages which can be used for deterrent purposes. These hostages — the direct investment, the markets, the sources of raw materials — as the Arabs surely know, can be dealt with much more flexibly in economic deterrent relationships than populations can in military deterrent relationships. First, the threat to such economic stakes is not suicidal; it is therefore by no means incredible. Second, the hostages in question are within the territory of the deterror, not the territory of the deterree. They are therefore subject to a much wider range of persuasion and influence than the population of an opposing state.

Many have failed to see that the extensive American direct investment in Western Europe provides hostages which can be influenced by community-wide policy developed by the EEC. The great American stake in the West European economy provides enormous leverage to European political leaders. In much the same fashion the large Japanese direct investment in the United States represents a stake in the American economy which American leaders can seek to affect. Of the non-communist industrial nations only Japan has failed to acquire economic hostages which it might seek to influence to produce more cooperative behaviour on the part of its trading associates. It has held down industrial imports and has refused to permit any substantial direct

27

investment in its enterprises. Perhaps not surprisingly Japan has been somewhat less effective than other major states in international economic negotiations.

Economic deterrent mechanisms can also *not* be used in the case of the communist countries because, to the present at least, they have not developed any substantial stake in Western industrial economies. They do not offer hostages which Europe, Japan or the United States could exert pressure upon to promote cooperative behaviour. They also lack the ability to influence non-communist developed countries by such techniques. They have not permitted Western nations and Japan to develop much of a stake in their economies, though the stake may grow with time. Soviet raw material supplies are very attractive to the non-communist industrial nations; and it may be that Western technology still has attractions for Russian leaders. If so, reciprocal stakes of mutual interest might develop in the future. For the moment, however, military deterrence is the crude but apparently necessary means of safeguarding tolerable relations between East and West.

It is therefore difficult to accept either the pessimistic or the optimistic forecasts of the amount of cooperation which can generally be expected in world political relationships. Certainly, the optimistic notion that states will cooperate because they will suffer if they do not, is far from being universally true. On the other hand, it simply is not true that international relations is a state of war and that there are no means of bringing about cooperation short of war. Agreements may not be enforced by a superior power, but they are often adhered to nonetheless. States recognise that they may not escape unscathed from the consequences of their own uncooperative acts. Both military deterrence and to an increasing degree economic deterrence have made possible a substantial regulation of the system by states themselves. The development of economic interdependence has if anything strengthened this tendency because it has provided industrial states with the means by which to make regulation effective. The increasing 'stake' which developed economies have in each other's well-being will make mutual regulation of behaviour even more powerful in the future than it has been in the past.

This conclusion is somewhat more optimistic than pessimistic. But it does not mean that the form of interdependence in the international system will inexorably be positive, with the interests of one state very nearly coinciding with the interests of another. Indeed, the new regulative mechanism which interdependence helps to provide may not always be used. If used, the result could at least conceivably be greater conflict rather than accommodation and eventual cooperation. If the threat of coercion must lie behind each cooperative agreement, there will be some occasions in which coercion will be returned for coercion and conflict will follow. Thus in strictly legal terms Hobbes was right: since there is no enforceable law in international relations, enforcement by one state cannot be legally differentiated from *ex parte* hostile action. The Balance of Power probably prevented wars in the nineteenth century, but who is to say that it never caused war? The attempt to restrain a power seeking predominance can be viewed as a hostile act, requiring hostile action in return. In the 1930s economic deterrent mechanisms utterly failed to bring about cooperation among states. When one state sought to discipline or restrain another, this led simply to another round of tariffs, depreciations or exclusionary quotas. In the end, all nations suffered greatly.

It is therefore uncertain today that the present tools of enforcement of cooperation will in fact procure cooperation and not conflict. The greater interdependence of international relations in both military and economic realms means that the stakes are much higher, the consequences of conflict much more pervasive and catastrophic. But it does not follow that conflict will never occur and that the apparatus of contemporary international cooperation will be maintained indefinitely.

The Significance of the Oil Crisis

The oil crisis is the kind of issue which could cause a breakdown in the structure of Western economic cooperation. The consequences for non-communist industrial economies are enormous, and there is a very great temptation to acquire adequate oil supplies by separate bilateral deals with the Arab producers. The nature of pre-existing Western industrial cooperation should however be roughly sketched as a basis for considering the impact of the oil weapon. Between 1960 and August 1971 the salient fact of the industrial world's economy was the United States' deficit. This deficit made it possible for Europe and Japan to run surpluses, and as long as the dollar was the major reserve currency neither American nor European growth was greatly hampered. The United States could print dollars to finance its deficit. This favourable situation was only possible because West European and Japanese central banks were willing to hold dollars in payment for the American debt; they did not insist, in the large, on repayment in gold or in changing their dollar balances into gold. If they had done so, the US gold stock would immediately have disappeared.

After August 1971, the dollar was no longer the major reserve currency in world trade. It would no longer confidently be held by creditors. Nations therefore sought to acquire other currencies to hedge their bets against depreciation. But the collapse of the dollar cut into the European and Japanese surplus. The devaluation of the dollar meant that Washington would now eliminate its balance of payments deficit. That objective has finally been achieved. But the elimination of the American deficit could only take place at the expense of Canada, European nations and Japan, the main trading partners of the United States. It therefore was necessary for a number of other nations to float their currencies, or at least to prevent further upward revaluation. Britain and Italy were not strong enough to join the deutschmark anchored European 'snake'; France had to sever ties with it. The Japanese have brought the value of the yen down. But the important point is that since most surpluses and deficits were won or lost in trade with other developed non-communist countries, there could be plenty of give and take in the process. One might even argue that the surpluses and deficits of Western countries have largely cancelled out because they are largely owed to each other. This does not mean that no surpluses or deficits were maintained with other parts of the globe. Up to recently, there had been a small deficit with the Middle Eastern countries, and a fair-sized surplus with the rest of the less developed countries.

The overall surplus with the rest of the world may perhaps seem odd. Why could not the raw materials and primary producing countries achieve favourable terms of trade with the industrial producers? There were two reasons for this. First, some industrial countries like the United States and Canada were also producers of agricultural surpluses and raw materials. Their own supplies of many of the critical items produced by one-crop or one-mineral economies helped to keep world prices down. Second and more important, no effective cartel arrangements had been made in the agricultural or raw material sectors. The competition among suppliers thus drove prices down.

This situation, as we know, has now greatly changed. Huge surpluses will now be earned by Middle Eastern oil producing countries. If current oil prices continue, the import bill for Western Europe, the United States and Japan, will be of the order of $40-60 billions higher per year. This amount of money is staggering. Some, like Secretary of State Kissinger, believe that the industrial countries cannot pay it and that prices must be brought down. But reduction is certainly not immediately in prospect and some oil experts think the price could go higher still. Spot prices for auctioned oil have ranged from $15-20 a barrel; far higher than the posted price for Saudi Arabian light of $11.65 per barrel. By the mid-eighties Western countries will have available large stocks of synthetic crudes produced from tar sands and shale. The exploitation of these deposits will probably reduce the longer term price to about $5-8 per barrel. But for the next ten years, Middle Eastern prices will govern all others. The problem which the non-communist industrial countries therefore confront is how these enormous sums can be paid.

If one thinks for a moment of the means by which West Germany or Japan have typically acquired their surpluses, it is clear that these methods and sources offer no solution to the problem of Arab oil costs. While some portion of Western surpluses have been gained in trade with the less developed countries, the really large surpluses have come from trade among developed countries themselves. Further and more importantly, the Western countries offer large markets in which surpluses could at least theoretically be earned. With the very limited export capacity of less developed states, they could in most cases not import the great quantities of goods from the West that would be necessary for industrial nations to earn the money to pay for oil. Even if they did, the transaction would yield greater supplies of the currency of developing nations, and it is very unlikely that the Middle Eastern producers would accept much of it in payment for their oil.

At first glance it therefore appears that industrial nations must earn the surpluses at the expense of each other. But they cannot do so as a group. If one nation is in surplus, another is in deficit. If all developed states try to do so, moreover, the world will return to the 'beggar my neighbour' policies of the 1930s and worse. Some nations will be quite unable to pay for their oil. Thus the Arab oil problem seems to turn the West against itself and to propose cannibalisation as a solution. This is the spectre which contemporary interdependence proffers and which will have to be exorcised by collective planning and action. If it is not, the world will witness the development of an interdependence of adversaries.

Fortunately, there are other solutions to the problem, though none of them are entirely satisfactory. The Arabs might be asked to hold Western currencies in payment for the oil. But currencies, as the last twenty years show, often depreciate. Since at least temporary floating is the typical present remedy for balance of payments ills, it would be difficult to convince the oil producing countries that Western currencies would retain their value. The inflationary trends which have afflicted every industrial country, moreover, could affect even a composite basket of the world's strongest currencies. This would present a special problem for Arab economic ministers because, at a certain point, the oil will be more valuable in the ground. Over the next decade oil is not likely to be a depreciating asset. Why should the Middle Eastern oil producers accept depreciating assets in return for a possibly appreciating asset? One answer to this problem might be to seek to tie oil prices to the depreciation of Western currencies, allowing the producers a higher price as currencies declined in value. But this would only accentuate the problem that the surpluses already create. Then the industrial countries would have to earn more abroad to pay for oil imports.

The simplest solution perhaps would be for the Arab nations and Iran to import such a large quantity of industrial goods that these imports would balance the oil exports. But at the moment that is impossible. The Arab nations with small populations and sparsely settled desert areas, cannot absorb such new infusions. They appear to have little potential for substantial industrial and economic development in the short run. Indeed, over the past ten years or so, the most optimistic measure of the ability to absorb imports is only half as large as the quantity of exports.

An ideal solution from the humanitarian point of view would be to use their currency surpluses for investment in the less developed countries of Asia, Africa and Latin America. In some cases the absorptive capacity of such countries is high, and economic development might follow. The investment and development would give rise to a much larger market for Western industrial imports, thus allowing the industrial nations to earn the wherewithal to pay for Arab oil. This solution, however, might not wholly solve the problem. It is very likely that the Arab nations will invest in African countries partly to express their gratitude for African solidarity with the Arab cause during the Yom Kippur war. But it is not likely that they would make such substantial investments that the amounts would generate industrial exports large enough to pay for Western oil imports. The returns on investment in the less developed countries would be very small at first and from the Arab point of view they would have to hold on to their investments for a very long term to make them pay. Even then, there would be the question whether such investments would offer a greater return than untapped oil supplies in their own countries. It is probably not to be expected then, that any large portion of the oil revenues will be invested in the developing countries.

Alternatively, of course, one might invest directly in Western industrial economies. The return on investments here would probably be higher at least in the short run. If any one industrial country, such as Japan or the United States, were to be the favoured location for Arab funds, however, the steady accumulation of American or Japanese productive assets in Arab hands could pose important internal political problems. Further, while investment would represent the return of funds and therefore cancel the deficit to the Middle East for the countries selected, other industrial countries would have to earn surpluses on their own. How could they be sure of doing so?

A better solution would be Arab investments in the entire range of industrial economies. A diversified basket of investments would assuage the problem of special treatment for some countries. But investment itself raises difficulty in the Arab world. The oil producing nations have at least until recently preferred to acquire liquid capital and to keep their funds in banks. They might then capitalise upon shifts in currency values. But the very liquidity of Arab capital and its transit from market to market greatly complicates the present problem of vast and sudden flows of capital. The huge amounts at Arab disposal will make this problem much more acute in the future than it has been in the past. Such unequilibrated flows could completely upset the international monetary system.

In the end it appears likely that some combination of uses for Arab funds will be found. Some will probably be held in a variety of currencies; some will be ploughed into investment in industrial nations. Some will be spent on imports and investment in their own countries and in Africa. The oil producers know that demands for certain forms of payment could undermine Western economies and precipitate a depression, which in turn would cause a collapse of oil prices. They do not wish to push beyond the limit of the resiliency of industrial economies, but they wish to extract as much as they can while their oil has absolutely unique value.

The importance of the oil crisis is that it is a kind of litmus paper test of future interdependence in the Western world. Each nation may try to solve the problem itself, and bilateral deals exchanging arms for oil supplies are to be expected. Japan and a number of Western countries may be expected to try to develop special relationships with individual Arab producers, safeguarding their access to oil supplies. But it seems highly unlikely that each nation can provide for necessary supplies on its own. If one nation seeks to do so, it may be forced to try to acquire surpluses at the expense of its European, American or Japanese colleagues. Unless this effort takes place with the agreement of others in the context of a common plan, it could be self-defeating. All states cannot run surpluses at each other's expense.

Thus some general agreement among industrial nations about the means they will use to pay for Arab oil is absolutely mandatory. The Arabs also must agree that the plan gives them a reasonable return for their oil, and that the assets they acquire will not be subject to continued depreciation. Such agreement has not been found among Western and industrial nations. Western hesitation and uncertainty over this problem offers profound grounds for doubt about the future state of economic interdependence among industrial nations. It is at least conceivable that major economic conflicts among industrial states could take place. It is therefore far too early to state categorically that increased interdependence will assume cooperative form.

The conclusion that one must reach both theoretically and practically is that of a Scottish verdict. The proponents of transnationalism and high interdependence as boons to international cooperation and peace have by no means proved their case. The pessimists have not been proved right, but they still could be right. In all probability the issue has not yet been decided by the determinism of social scientific arguments; governments still possess a latitude to control their fates if they will but seize upon it. The unresolved question today is whether they still have the political will to find a solution.

2 TRANSNATIONAL AND TRANSGOVERNMENTAL RELATIONS

Joseph S. Nye

My subject within the series topic of New Dimensions of World Politics is the role of transnational and transgovernmental relations.[1] My talk might be subtitled 'Beyond the billiard ball concept of the nation state'. Those who think that I am addressing a straw man I could refer to a popular text book in which you will find little circles and little arrows between the circles as an aid to understanding international politics. In any case, whatever one thinks of visual aids, the dominant paradigm that has informed the discipline of international politics since the 1940s and 1950s has been a 'state-centric realism' based on three powerful simplifying assumptions: (1) significant relations between states; (2) states act as coherent units; (3) political-military security concerns are the dominant objectives and motivations of states. In Professor Morgenthau's words, 'two factors are the basis of international society. The multiplicity and antagonism of its elements, the nations.' Or in the view of the sensitive French writer, Raymond Aron, there are two archetypical actors in international politics, the soldier and the diplomat.[2]

Obviously there is no single school called 'state-centric realism' and there are important differences among authors which are of considerable importance when we get down to details. For example Morgenthau tends to regard the basis of the states' concern with security as stemming from man's will to power whereas others see it more as stemming from anarchy, the absence of a common sovereign. They share, however, a Hobbesian view of the world in which the central problem is insecurity, war and resort to force. The new wave of scientific approaches to international politics has tended to incorporate the traditional assumptions of state-centric realism. William Coplin and colleagues, in a recent survey of articles in the behavioural school, found that nearly all shared the assumptions of the dominant approach. Coplin titled his paper 'Colour it Morgenthau'.[3]

How realistic are the three assumptions? If we look at East-West relations between communist and western countries, there is a great deal of validity in the assumption. Communist states do tend to act more as units. Statesmen are concerned with balancing power. Security and potential military conflict are central elements in the relations between the superpowers. Even in this area, however, it is worth noticing the role of transnational relations. Such questions as joint ventures between multinational enterprises and Eastern European governments; the treatment of intellectuals in the USSR; and the question of Jewish emigration have become entwined with more traditional issues in the strange politics of partial 'détente'. If we turn to other areas of global politics, the three 'realist' assumptions are not as realistic as the name seems to imply. Indeed they may divert attention away from important questions. In North-South relations, for example, realist assumptions often lead to descriptions of third world areas as 'power vacuums' and to predictions of large powers being 'sucked in' militarily. Realism tends to neglect the informal pattern of dependence that is often maintained by coalitions formed between parts of third world countries and parts of rich countries — what Johann Galtung has called 'structural imperialism'.[4]

It is when we look at relations amongst the advanced industrial societies, however, that the state-centric realist assumptions are most misleading. Henry Kissinger's description of a world based on a five power balance is a very misleading image. Japan and the European community are not similar to the United States and the Soviet Union. What you really have is a structure of two triangles; a military triangle composed of China, the United States and the Soviet Union; and an economic triangle composed of Japan, the United States and Europe.[5] It is rather elementary geometry that two triangles do not make a pentagon, but equally important is the fact that international relations within the economic triangle of advanced industrial nations do not conform to the balance of power image.

If we go beyond imagery and ask 'what's going on in world politics today?' we find that these state-centric realist assumptions are not very helpful in understanding a number of characteristics. Let me list six. The list is not exclusive. You can probably think of others. The list is merely to give you some flavour of what is happening in world politics and why scholars and practitioners (including scholars who have become practitioners) cannot afford to limit their perceptions by the three traditional assumptions.

First, let us consider the changing role of military force. Military force has become more costly for large states, particularly nuclear states. It is less useful in particular for the achievement of positive goals, particularly in the economic area. A century ago when the United States wanted to make Japan trade with it, it threatened bombardment. Last year when the United States wanted the Japanese to revalue the yen, bombardment was not a very useful option. Why has there been a change in the role of military force? There is a considerable and interesting literature on this.[6] One of the most important reasons is the role of nuclear weapons which has introduced a disproportion between ends and means and huge risks in calculations. The dangers of escalation to nuclear confrontation are often a deterrent against action by nuclear powers. Second, nationalism plays an important role. Rule over socially mobilised populations is far more costly than it was in colonial days. Third, there are internal restraints in western societies. An ethic of antimilitarism intensely held by part of the population in the West has to some extent put a higher cost on the use of force by political leaders. Causation is a complex question and there is much more to be said than can be covered here. Technology may be making force more easily available, for example, to small states and nonstate actors. Our point is merely that there has been a change and that as force is devalued other forms of power become more important.

A second characteristic is the increased role of communications across borders. There has been an increased rapidity and sensitivity in transborder communications. At the trivial level it is intriguing to see how quickly a social fad like 'streaking' spread among Western societies. More seriously, it is remarkable how quickly a new issue like ecology has boomed across international borders, boomed in part through the help of the Club of Rome, a very small transnational elite group. Morgenthau is probably correct that there is no such thing as world opinion in the singular, but there are transnational opinions in the plural. Analogous elites such as students, racial groups and military officers with similar roles and functions in different societies are much more quickly aware of each other's positions, tactics and doings than they were half a century ago.

A third characteristic is the degree of government involvement in the provision of economic welfare. In nearly all societies today welfare objectives have become more important to governments. 'Consumerism' is a dominant ideology, and governments are being held responsible for the economic welfare of their people in a much more direct sense than they were fifty years ago. Governments try to control the economy more, and this leads to a paradox. Before World War I there were few overt governmental controls on transactions across borders or interferences with the market mechanism, but this did not lead to as great a degree of political sensitivity and *policy* interdependence as in the regulated world that we live in today. In other words, under *laissez faire* there was *societal* interdependence, but governments were not held as fully responsible for socioeconomic change as today. Now governments are held more accountable for welfare, and the policy measures by which they try to cope with transactions across borders, create an inter-dependence of *policy*. A policy change may be nullified by another government's policy. Success becomes contingent upon the actions of another government. So as governments have tried to control transactions and to cut down on societal interdependence, they have found themselves enmeshed in a greater degree of policy interdependence.

A fourth characteristic, in part a product of the others, is the increase in the number of issues in international politics. The agenda of relations between states today is full of issues that were not there before. Most obvious, with the oil crisis filling the headlines, is the increased prominence of economic issues, but also important are issues like ecology, space communications, the deep seabed, food and population. I might even note that American relations with Turkey have been highly influenced by the problem of the poppy in the last few years because of the taste amongst some middleclass youth for a poppy derivative.

39

A fifth characteristic is the increased role of nonstate actors which in a sense could be said to have private foreign policies of their own. The most dramatic of these are the multinational enterprises which are now receiving a good deal of attention from national governments and from the United Nations. Multinational enterprises can play direct and indirect roles in international politics. The direct role can be best illustrated by the dramatic example of ITT in Chile. The indirect role occurs when corporations do not have a policy toward a given government but pursue policies and actions which have strong effects on governments. A good example of this would be the transfer of funds in which corporate treasuries acting rationally and reading signals the same way can put the finance ministers of the major nations on the run over a weekend.

A sixth characteristic is the management of foreign policy. Aron says that international politics is the domain of the diplomat and the soldier, but who are the diplomats and what are the soldiers doing? Gordon Craig has described the classical diplomacy of an earlier period as follows: 'with the essential facts at their disposal and provided further with such time honoured rules of thumb as *ragione di stato* and *balance of power,* the diplomats possessed a conceptual framework within which they could move with confidence'.[7] But this is a world that has now departed. Today there is an overshadowing of foreign offices as societies interact with each other at many points that cannot be easily controlled. There are direct contacts among what were once considered domestic bureaucracies of different governments. Foreign offices cannot hope fully to monitor the range of direct contacts among governments of advanced industrial societies. This creates tremendous difficulties of maintaining policy coherence.

These are six illustrations of some characteristics of present world politics which are not very well caught by the classical assumptions of state-centric realism. They bring to mind a conference which I attended two years ago on 'Trends in World Politics'. If you could summarise the discussion in a phrase that phrase would be 'the interpenetration of domestic and international politics'. The autonomy of domestic politics and international politics in their own spheres was no longer as great as it once had been. As one of my colleagues who earned his Ph.D. only fifteen years ago contemplated this summary, he complained rather plaintively that it meant that his graduate training was obsolete. There is still a good deal of this obsolescence in graduate training, reflected in the way that domestic politics and international politics are kept separate. Domestic politics is often treated as a process within a Lockean community in which the concern is with consensus and the legitimacy of established institutions. International politics is treated as a Hobbesian world where sovereign states form alliances and concern themselves solely with the balance of power [If you are modern and behavioural, you talk about systems of states]. James Rosenau put this well when he said that comparative and international politics have been kept apart not by mutual antagonism but by reciprocal boredom. Each has its own conceptual jail. International politics has a conceptual jail called 'national interest' which allows students of international politics to view all policies as similarly motivated. Comparative politics has a conceptual goal called 'the national system' which assumes that the ultimate master of all that transpires within national boundaries is part of the national system.[8]

There has been a change or the beginnings of change in the study of international politics in the last few years. A number of people have been dissatisfied with traditional assumptions about the subject. I will not try to survey all the various dissatisfactions this evening, but will talk about the work that Robert Keohane and I have done on transnational and transgovernmental relations.[9] In a very broad sense, there are relations across state borders that are not controlled by the central executive or foreign policy organs of governments. *Transnational* interactions involve at least one actor that is not a government. Let me give you a few examples. ITT in Chile, mentioned earlier, would be a good transnational interaction. So also was the action of the Ford Foundation in Brazil, when it developed an institute which provided a way for Brazilian intellectuals who were thrown out of their universities to continue to work in Brazil. Guerrillas hijacking an aeroplane or kidnapping an ambassador or a foreign businessman are also involved in transnational interactions. Scientists communicating at a Pugwash meeting; Israelis raising funds in the United States; and labour unions acting in less developed countries to raise the level of wages and thereby prevent jobs from being exported from rich countries are examples.

41

Obviously, we have used a very broad definition of transnational interaction. By now you might be saying to yourself that I, standing here, am a transnational actor. That is true but I should point out to you that I am a politically trivial one. One can introduce a *de minimus* clause to protect against devaluation of a definition.

The second category I would like to sketch here for you is *transgovernmental* interactions. These are direct interactions among subunits of different governments that are not closely controlled or guided by policies of the cabinets of chief executives of the governments. Let me give three examples to illustrate this definition.

First, there is the weather bureau case between the United States and Canada in the early 1960s.[10] The American weather bureau wanted a certain allocation of radio frequencies for meteorological research. In normal bureaucratic politics, they got into a dispute with other parts of the U.S. government on how these frequencies would be allocated, and lost the dispute. Rather than accept defeat, the head of the U.S. weather bureau called his counterpart in Ottawa and said in effect, 'Do you realise the terrible thing that has been done to our mutual interests as weather bureaux? Can't you do something about it from your side?' So the Canadian weather bureau took the initiative in getting the Canadian government to take the 'proper' position. Canada subsequently lead a successful coalition in international bargaining and the U.S. government was outvoted. The weather bureaux won over the Defense Department of the White House. This is an example of a transgovernmental coalition, with government actors in two different countries who have a mutuality of interest and coordinate their behaviour to promote the mutual interest, which is not necessarily the same as that defined at the top of their own governments.

Another example is the famous Sky Bolt affair, described in Richard Neustadt's book. *Alliance Politics.* Thorneycroft, the British Defence Minister at the time, did not have clear forewarning that the United States was going to cancel the Sky Bolt missile out from under him. McNamara, the American Secretary of Defense at the time, had been inhibited from giving a clear warning to Thorneycroft because the American Air Force and Royal Air Force had such very good contacts at the bureaucratic level. If McNamara had given full information to

Thorneycroft, the information would have got to the Royal Air Force. The RAF would then have told the USAF, who would then have appealed to their allies in Congress to prevent McNamara from taking Sky Bolt out of his budget. In other words, transgovernmental communication at the bureaucratic level, which McNamara feared, had the effect of drying up communication at the higher level.[11]

A third example is the reversion of Okinawa to Japan. It had been American policy to give Okinawa back to the Japanese government, but it was one of those policies which nobody was in any hurry to do anything about. An official in the American Defense Department, foreseeing the rise of a number of frictions with the Japanese, feared that Okinawa might become a major issue that could poison U.S.-Japanese relations. He went to a Japanese counterpart at a similar level and advised him on how to word and route a message to the U.S. – government that would precipitate the right kind of policy response. This was a case of transgovernmental agenda setting.

These two categories of transnational interactions and transgovernmental interactions correspond to a relaxation of the assumptions that states are the only actors and that states act as units. There is an objection to relaxing these assumptions which must have occurred to many of you already. If international politics is hard to understand with 130 states, it becomes almost impossible to understand if you have to add all these extra actors. The traditional approach is parsimonious and the transnational approach is not. If a person can adequately predict and explain international politics while theorising from his armchair without doing research on transnational and transgovernmental actors, then his armchair is far less costly and should have the preference. This general objection takes several specific forms. One is the argument that 'this is very interesting but rather trivial because when you get down to the crunch, when you get down to an open public clash, governments always win'. Fortunately for us, that is not always true. There are examples that Keohane and I cite in our book where coalitions of airlines, for example, have in fact defeated governments. But even if it were true that governments win open dramatic clashes, the question is whether those open dramatic clashes are a good representation of the whole political process. I would argue that they are not; that open and dramatic clashes are a very rare type of case. Most governments tend to compromise before things get to the open and dramatic stage. What you want to think about is how much has the cost of reaching a solution that a government prefers been raised by the action of various transnational actors?

The second form of objection is that transnational relations do not affect high politics. They affect functional areas such as money or trade, but not high politics. The trouble with this objection is knowing what 'high politics' is. People who make this objection often slide back and forth between two different definitions. 'High politics' may refer to the level in the government at which an issue is dealt with. If a president deals with something it is high politics. But then you find that presidents are spending a lot of their time thinking about economic matters. President de Gaulle was an exception and used to dismiss such matters with the phrase 'the baggage train will trail along'. Eventually in 1968 it was the baggage train that helped to defeat him. The objection is not impressive if high politics is defined by level. Alternatively high politics may refer not to level, but to the types of issues that kings used to deal with, that is war and high diplomacy. Then high politics is not a level but a type; it has to do with military and security matters. Defined this way, the argument that transnational relations do not affect high politics tends to ignore the very real linkage between economic and security questions. To say that there is no relation between troops in Europe today and trade and monetary negotiations is a fundamental misunderstanding of the attitude of the American Congress and of world politics more generally.

The third objection is that transnational relations are not new. This is true. But if it is true, then that makes the criticism that much more damning to the traditional realist assumptions. Moreover, there have been changes which have increased the importance of transnational relations both in the sensitivity and rapidity of communications which I mentioned earlier, and in the growth and the scale of transnational organisations. There is very little similarity between the old East India Company and IBM. IBM has much greater flexibility.

Despite my criticism of the objections, I want to make it clear that parsimony is a powerful criterion for the construction of theory and that the choice about approaching problems with state-centric assumptions is not necessarily an either/or proposition. You should first try to explain things in the simplest possible terms, using powerful assumptions. Then if you feel you cannot adequately explain behaviour you must relax assumptions and look at nongovernmental and subgovernmental actors. Sometimes the work that Keohane and I have done is interpreted as saying that nongovernmental forces are taking over from governments and that the world is going to be ruled by nongovernmental forces. That interpretation is not only inaccurate, but I think it is nonsense. We are sceptical of the views of strong functionalists who believe that world politics is progressing to a nongovernmental utopia.

The other thing that I would like to make clear is that transnational relations is not a theory. It is an appeal for a broadening of scope of attention, for a broader paradigm, but you will have noticed that we defined transnational relations as residual categories and one does not theorise in terms of residual categories. By the term 'theory', I mean a coherent set of general propositions used as principles of explanation for a broader class of phenomena. Theory can be deductive or inductive. Deductive theory involves: (1) a set of assumptions; (2) theorems logically deduced from the assumptions and (3) falsifiable predictions from theorems. Inductive theory or what Stanley Hoffmann has called 'middle level theory' refers to empirically based generalisations which subsume broad categories of phenomena with *ceteris paribus* clauses carefully stated.[13]

A plea for greater attention to transnational relations does not prejudge the choice of type of theory one uses. If one leans toward a deductive theory you can apply theories of collective goods and political entrepreneurship. If one has an inductivist temperament, one can work with middle level theories of integration and interdependence. A choice among dependent variables is similarly open. One can choose to look at interstate relations: how do transnational relations affect the relations amongst states? One can choose to focus on a single state's foreign policy: how do transnational and transgovernmental relations affect its foreign policy? Or one can focus on something which has been greatly neglected by the traditional study of international politics − the allocation of values regardless of effects on interstate relations. Who gets what? After all, if you are a Philippine peasant whose child has died of a rather simple curable disease because the local doctor has emigrated to San Francisco where he can get a higher salary, it makes much more difference to you that there be something done about the 'brain drain', than that there be nuclear deterrence. It is just as much a matter of life and death. Many of the criticisms that radicals have raised in the last few years about the sterility of the study of international politics have been valid. We have not spent enough time looking at political factors that affect the allocation of values. Another point in favour of the broader transnational paradigm is the greater likelihood of attention to such questions and the flexibility in setting the dependent variables.

I indicated above that integration and interdependence theories can be used in conjunction with a transnational paradigm. In the 1950s one of the challenges to state-centric realism grew out of the work of people who were studying the European unity movement. Scholars like Karl Deutsch and Ernst Haas argued that European interstate politics was not explainable simply as a balancing of power. There were also internal dynamics which involved other actors besides states. The interaction of state and nonstate groups in economic and political matters was affecting the relation of states, and was not caught by traditional realist assumptions. Integration theory became a respected but rather encapsulated part of the field of international politics. This was for two reasons: first, it was too regional; and second, it was too teleological. There were too many assumptions about purposes and progress towards a united Europe, or united Central America or united Africa, and this left the approach open to critics. In addition, the situation of integration theory was in part the fault of the dominant realist paradigm model. Integration theory just did not fit with the rest of the assumptions of the paradigm and during the Cold War period that was the way reality seemed to be. So integration theory was treated as a capsule and left as an odd area unto itself.[15]

Integration theory can be adapted and mined to provide insights about the major issues of world politics today, particularly those among the advanced industrial societies. First let me say that there are two ways of making integration theory more relevant with which I do not agree. One view was that there would be a spread of regional integration.

schemes, and that therefore to understand regional integration would be to understand much of world politics. Ernst Haas tended to suggest this in 1961.[16] This is just not the way the world turned out to be. The second approach was the focus on global integration. The uniting of the world would be analogous to the uniting of Europe.[17] Robert Angell's book *Peace on the March* for example tends to make this kind of argument. I am rather sceptical about it. In my view, integration theory must first be shorn of its regional and teleological assumptions. Then there are five major contributions to international relations theory which one can distill from integration theory and which are the types of middle level theoretical propositions which can be developed and applied within the broader transnational paradigm.

First is analysis by issue area. World politics is not a seamless web. In the analysis of domestic politics, this has been conventional wisdom for some time. Robert Dahl's study of New Haven, Connecticut, for example, found that the power elite on one issue was not necessarily the power elite on the other. Politics varied by issue area. In the mid-sixties, James Rosenau suggested that this insight be applied to international politics.[18] The area where empirical work was done on variance by issue area was in studies of regional integration. The emphasis on the sectoral approach to integration led to a concern with politics of different issue areas. For example, Lindberg and Scheingold's comparison of European integration in agriculture and transport found differences in the structure of groups and differences in type of leadership leading to different outcomes.[19] Translating that to international politics more broadly, one would expect to find differences in the politics of money, trade, shipping, petroleum and air transport. Each issue has different transnational actors and different governmental bureaucracies involved. These actors have different power assets, and national patterns of outcomes are not the same in all areas. Thus one of the insights that can be developed from integration theory, is analysis by issue area and comparison of issue areas over time and across issue areas.

Second is the question of linkage. Though world politics is not a seamless web, at some level obviously all issues do relate. One of the key strategies of the integrationists in Europe was to spread integration from sector to sector. The problem was whether the linkage process or 'spill over' would overcome the functional autonomy of different sectors. Statesmen and bureaucrats tried to manipulate these links.

This linkage among issue areas has not been much studied in world politics. Henry Kissinger is known to have stated that in the relations between the United States and the Soviet Union all issues were linked. Yet in fact it seems that issues were not linked the same way. It was quite possible to have trade talks and to bomb Hanoi at the same time. If you look at the relationship between the United States and Canada, one of the intriguing things is that overt linkage is diplomatically taboo and this tends to strengthen the position of the weaker state. We should know more about who links whom and how successfully in world politics. What is the role, for instance, of legislators, of private groups, of different bureaucracies in creating or weakening linkages? This is another area where we need much more work in international politics and can take a lead from integration theory.

A third insight is the question of politicisation and depoliticisation. In integration and regional integration theory there was a feeling that integration became more controversial as it involved a broader range of actors and as it reached higher levels of political actors over time. Indeed strategies were based on this. The neo-functionalist strategy of Jean Monnet and his colleagues aimed at working from a depoliticised early stage to a more politicised late stage. The federalist approach on the contrary was to start highly politicised.[20] Applied to world politics more generally, a concern for politicisation leads to devoting more attention to agenda formation. Why do some issues get attention and others do not? If a president's attention is diverted from one issue rather than another, that may be as important an aspect of power as having an input in the decision once the agenda is set. The question of agenda formation is the question of the emergence of new issues. Who tends to put issues on the agenda and who tries to keep them off? How do they get politicised and depoliticised? This is a set of questions where international political analysis has been lacking.

The fourth insight from integration theory that can be applied more widely within a transnational framework, relates to the units of analysis. I have already said a bit about this. When we talk about interdependence among states we often neglect the fact that there is a different type of interdependence between particular groups within states. Two states may be interdependent in one way and two groups within the states may be interdependent in quite another way. For example, the US and the Soviet Union are highly interdependent in the military area, but with negative connotations. The U.S. and Soviet airforces are interdependent in quite a different way. Their internal bureaucracy benefits from the interdependence. To take a nongovernmental example, U.S. farmers and European consumers have the same interests and are interdependent, with a positive sign, while U.S. farmers and European farmers are interdependent with a more negative sign. So when we think about interdependence in world politics it is important to keep our units of analysis clear and not just look at state to state interdependence.

It is worth noticing that you get different possibilities for transgovernmental interaction depending on whether one puts the Ministers of Agriculture together or puts the American Minister of Agriculture together with the European Minister of Finance. Thinking in nonstate units of analysis while approaching questions of how to structure multibureaucratic decision making is another important insight to be derived from integration theory.[21]

That leads to my fifth point, the significance of international institutions. Under state-centric realist assumptions, there is very little role for international organisation. After all, if one phrases the question as 'Will international organisations be given enough power to have supranationality?', then it does not look as though there is much hope. Since nation-states act in self-interest, there is little role for international organisation. But that realist view begs two important questions; what is the 'self' and which 'interest'? International organisations can affect which 'self' and which 'interest' prevails. International organisation helps to set the arena. If a group of people meet together in one arena, the political outcome may be very different than if they meet together in another. Take an example from the Law of the Sea conference. When marine scientists meet together in the International Oceanographic Commission, they tend to come up with outcomes that are close to scientists' preferences. When scientists meet in a larger arena with other interests such as shipping, defence and petroleum exploration represented, the scientists tend to rank pretty far down and the outcomes are likely to be less satisfactory. Choice of arena can have an enormous effect on the outcome.

International organisations also represent a point of political intervention in transnational systems, and their secretariats a potential participant in transgovernmental coalitions. For example, Maurice Strong in the ecology area has tried to help develop organisations and bureaucracies which will have an interest in links with the Environment Secretariat.

In summary, I have argued that the broader paradigm of transnational relations combined with the development of theoretical insights derived from an integration theory shorn of its regional and teleological assumptions provides us with an interesting path to follow in trying to understand the complex aspects of world politics sketched above. I might mention in closing that I have not remained simply in the armchair but have recently worked on a study trying to apply this to the United States and Canada, a particularly interesting case because the United States and Canada is a situation where there are no threats of force; there is very asymmetrical interdependence; economic issues dominate the agenda; and transnational organisations are very important. Something like 60 per cent of Canadian manufacturing is owned from outside the country). Transgovernmental interaction is very important. There is a direct contact by phone between Ottawa and Washington. Some thirty agencies have direct contacts with each other. In 1968 a study was done that showed that of some 6,500 visits back and forth across the border by Canadian and American officials, only 139 of them involved the Department of External Affairs. The US and Canada is almost a limiting case for the type of politics which I have been describing. It is a topic which has been greatly ignored by most scholars of international politics. David Baldwin wrote not too long ago that Canadian-American relations tell us nothing about the big problems of world politics and Arnold Wolfers (one of the best of the traditional theorists) once wrote that the Canadian-American relationship was marked by an indifference to power.[22] This is an interesting example of how realist assumptions can blind even the most sensitive of scholars.

In my study, I took all cases of conflict between the United States and Canada which reached the president's attention, and compared the period 1920-39 with the postwar period, 1950-69.[23] The study showed that transnational relations of various types have always been important in forming the agenda. In the prewar period, there were eight cases of high-level conflict; six of these eight arose out of transnational relations. In the postwar period sixteen of thirty-one conflicts arose out of transnational relations. What changes between the two periods is the rise of transnational organisation. In the prewar period, one of the six cases arose from a transnational organisation's activities. In the postwar period nearly half did.

In terms of the political process − how things get worked out − transnational-transgovernmental relations were important in two out of eight prewar cases and in seventeen out of thirty-one postwar cases. So there is a considerable increase from a quarter to half of the postwar cases. As for variance by issue area, in the military issue area the United States came out ahead in four out of seven cases. In the economic issue area, the United States came out ahead in only three out of fifteen cases. On the question of whether transnational organisations benefit the home country (the United States in this case) against the host country, the answer is 'not necessarily'. In cases where this is not transnational or transgovernmental interaction, the Canadian came out ahead in five out of fourteen cases, roughly a third. In cases where there was an important transnational role the Canadians did better in four out of nine, nearly half. In cases with an important transgovernmental role, the Canadians came out ahead in five out of eight, more than half. I concluded from this that transnational organisations can support either a home or a host government. They are a third party with separate interests of their own and cannot be assumed to have the interest either of their home or the host government. They pick and choose as it suits their immediate interests. This somewhat cryptic report of results from a long study gives you some illustration of the fact that empirical work can be done along these lines I have suggested, and that the first of these efforts tends to substantiate the types of hypotheses which Keohane and I have argued in our earlier work.

In conclusion, I have argued that we need to broaden the scope of actors which we consider as important in international politics. We have to do this if we are to understand the interaction between domestic and international politics. A better understanding is important if we are going to cope with the world in which we are living. It is also important if we are going to pay more attention to the questions of distribution, and if we are going to be able justly to manage the interdependence which is growing in rather an uneven fashion. What I would like to leave with you is the belief that transnational relations are important but not that they are necessarily beneficial. Some may have very malign effects. They may in some cases have benign effects. There is nothing automatic or utopian about their growth. We need to learn more about transnational and transgovernmental relations if we are to cope with them. Otherwise, I go back to my original metaphor of 'beyond the billiard ball' and say that if we do not develop a better understanding of transnational relations we are going to remain in policy terms behind the eight ball.

References

1. This lecture is based on work done jointly with Robert O. Keohane of Stanford University.
2. Hans Morgenthau, *Politics Among Nations* (New York, 1967); Raymond Aron, *Peace and War* (New York, 1966).
3. Paper delivered at the International Studies Association (New York, 1973).
4. Johan Galtung, 'A Structural Theory of Imperialism', *Journal of Peace Research* (Oslo) 5: 375-95.
5. Zbigniew Brzezinski, 'The Balance of Power Delusion', *Foreign Policy* (Summer 1972).
6. See for example, International Institute for Strategic Studies, *Force in Modern Societies* (London: Adelphi Papers 102, 103, 1973). Our own views are more systematically elaborated in R.O. Keohane and J.S. Nye, 'World Politics and the International Economic System', in C. F. Bergsten (ed.), *The Future of International Economic Order* (Lexington, Mass., 1973).
7. Gordon Craig and Felix Gilbert, *The Diplomats, 1919-39* Vol. I (Princeton, 1953), p.4
8. *Linkage Politics* (New York, 1969), p.8.
9. *Transnational Relations and World Politics* (Cambridge, Mass., 1972).
10. See Edward L. Miles, 'Transnationalism in Space: Inner and Outer', in *Transnational Relations* (cited).
11. Richard Neustadt, *Alliance Politics* (New York, 1970), p.64.

12. Oran Young, 'The Perils of Odysseus: On Constructing Theories of International Relations', *World Politics,* XXIV (Spring 1972)
13. *Contemporary Theory in International Relations* (Englewood Cliffs, 1960).
14. Harrison Wagner, 'Dissolving the State', *International Organisation* Vol. 28, Summer 1974.
15. These views are elaborated in R.O. Keohane and J.S. Nye, 'International Interdependence and Integration', in Fred Greenstein and Nelson Polsby (eds.), *The Handbook of Political Science* (forthcoming). For a somewhat different approach, see Charles Pentland, *International Theory and European Integration* (London, 1973).
16. 'International Integration: the European and the Universal Process', *International Organization* (1961).
17. Richard Van Wagenen, 'The Concept of Community and the Future of the United Nations', *International Organization* (1965); Robert Angell, *Peace on the March* (Princeton, 1969).
18. James Rosenau, 'Foreign Policy as an Issue Area', *Domestic Sources of Foreign Policy.*
19. Leon Lindberg and Stuart Scheingold, *Europe's Would-Be Polity* (Englewood Cliffs, 1970).
20. This is elaborated in J.S. Nye, *Peace in Parts* (Boston, 1971).
21. This and the next point are developed in R.O. Keohane and J.S. Nye 'Transgovernmental Relations and World Politics', *World Politics* (October 1974).
22. David Baldwin, 'The Myth of the Special Relationship', in Stephen Clarkson (ed.), *An Independent Foreign Policy for Canada* (Toronto, 1968); Arnold Wolfers, *Discord and Collaboration* (Baltimore, 1962), p. 97
23. J.S. Nye, 'Transnational Relations and Interstate Conflict: An Empirical Analysis', *International Organization* (Autumn, 1974).

3 WORLD ORDER-KEEPING: SOME ALTERNATIVE STRUCTURES

George Modelski

Let me begin by explaining the title of this lecture. I regard order-keeping as a function assumed and performed in recent historical experience by the great powers and by the diplomatic and strategic complex associated with them. This structure I propose to look at with some care, describing it and assessing its impact on the world as accurately as I can and as perceptively as our theoretical equipment allows. But I shall also maintain that this structure is a changeable one, that it is changing and that it might even be amenable to deliberate modification.

My main theme will therefore be a theoretical exploration of a set of structures that might be assumed by the global order-keeping industry. This is the set defined by the number of producers, or production centres, characterising such an industry, that is to say, by its degree of power concentration. My choice of the term 'concentration' is, of course, deliberate; it is intended to inject into this discussion analogies derived from the study of economic organisation and of market structures, and the problem of industrial concentration that is so central to it.[1]

The State of World Power Concentration

A concept identifying one particular structure within this set of structures is multipolarity, recently much in vogue as a definition of the essence of contemporary movement in world politics.[2] As a means of determining the state of world power concentration I propose to ask the question: is the world today or is it becoming, multipolar? Multipolarity may be defined as a structural form of the global political system such that the number of power centres in it exceeds two but is not greater than ten. In other words it is one form of power concentration characterised by several rather than by *one* or by *many* power aggregations and it is also customarily distinguished from bipolarity, a system noted for the presence of *two* power centres. Those of you who have studied Aristotle's *Politics* will have noticed that the classification implied in the scheme I am putting forward here is derivatively Aristotelian, for it distinguishes among systems according to whether the number of units or power centres comprised in each is *one* or *few* or *many*. This is a very fundamental classification of political systems because it underlies the distinction between one man rule (or dictatorship), oligarchy and democracy. It is, of course, one of the basic classificatory schemes of political science.

In this conception the idea of power centres (and of the industries they form) has two elements or connotations. To me it suggests capacity, or organisation capable of projecting military power on a global scale, hence a focus on military power that is globally relevant. But it also alludes to elements of authority, legitimacy and consensus and to the acceptance of certain organisations as necessary elements of the world political system, hence it rests upon the recognition that factors of perception and value embodied in judgements about authority also have a bearing on the structure of politics and order-keeping. Still in the Aristotelian tradition, a judgement that a system is multipolar therefore also involves a decision that the number of those *entitled* to rule, that is the number of those legitimately expected to exert power on behalf of common goals, must be restricted to the few rather than granted to one or to the many. It is a familiar point although in: in international politics the element of capacity has traditionally been more prominent than that of legitimacy.

I have now defined multipolarity and, by implication, the other structural arrangements of world order-keeping included in the notion of multipolarity: on the one side, bipolarity and unipolarity and, on the other, indeed opposite to it, the dispersed or deconcentrated system. I have defined multipolarity as being a form of concentration of military as distinct from economic and other forms of power and as embodying some legitimate capacity for pursuing policies relevant to global order.

The basic determinants of this power are military forces in being and the services they are capable of rendering in a relatively short period of time, say a year. Hence a system may operationally be defined as multipolar if it comprises more than two unified military organisations (and not alliances) each accounting for at least five per cent of global military effort but not comprising a large or overwhelming share of it, say more than forty per cent. This is a working definition of multipolarity and of the other systems implied in it. Unfortunately there is no good way of measuring the shares of services, that is the quantity of public goods of security, defence and global order rendered by military organisations; military manpower figures or lists of particular weapons are not ideally suited for this rather broad purpose. Thus we really have no good means of judging world order effectiveness and its world distribution. All we have is some capacity to measure the budgetary cost of maintaining forces and it goes without saying that the costliness of a force is not necessarily the best indicator of its effectiveness. I shall, lacking a more precise yardstick, use world figures on military expenditure as a handy if somewhat crude means of gauging the state of world power concentration.

I do not propose to delve deeply into the methodology I have employed in reaching the conclusions that I am just about to give you. This is a question of some complexity I simply do not have the time to go into and you will forgive me for being simply declaratory on this matter. But, having confronted the concepts with the empirical data on military power distributions as defined by budgetary expenditures I have reached the following conclusions about structural conditions of world politics since World War II.

1. In the global system power is significantly concentrated. It is a system characterised by an extremely high degree of power concentration. A very small number of states account for the great bulk of power. Between 1948 and 1972, that is for a period of a quarter century, only two powers have consistently accounted for more than five per cent of the world military effort. Unsurprisingly these were the United States and the Soviet Union. Britain, China and France mostly averaged between two and five per cent – the higher values being observed early in this period. Only three or four other states added consistently more than one

per cent to the total global effort. In short therefore, the condition of multipolarity never obtained in the postwar period and power rested throughout overwhelmingly in two centres only. The system was therefore primarily bipolar.

2. Within this basic condition of bopolarity and judging from two separate sets of data,[3] the US held throughout this period a significant edge over all other states, deploying in 1952 and in 1953 (at the time of the Korean mobilisation) over fifty per cent of world military power and until 1970 always exerting more than forty per cent of it and often coming close to one half of the total effort. The Soviet Union by contrast, and judging this time from one set of data, remained for a number of years below the level of twenty-five per cent. On the basis of such information the system could legitimately be described as having inclined towards predominance. Contrary to the prevailing impression about the postwar period, I would therefore argue that a tendency towards unipolarity characterised it rather than straight bipolarity.

3. From data sources now available, and the likely rates of change in this field, there is little prospect for the rise of new power centres of global significance in the time span of a decade or so. At the present time China seems to be nearest to the five per cent limit, standing at 4.8 per cent in 1970; but this does not give it a global capacity even though it might serve as a regional counterweight to Soviet power. Neither Japan nor India belong to the global class either, as it might be estimated that in present-day conditions nothing less than an effort in the region of ten per cent of world total could put an aspiring government into this category. The only possible exception is, of course, the potential Europe of the Nine that in 1970 added up to about 11 per cent of world power but whose forces were not then nor are today unified enough to constitute a single power centre. At the present time Europe may not even be a regional counterweight to Soviet power; it might become a global power centre in future years but it also might not.

4. Two sets of available data lend support to a preliminary conjecture that a long term trend towards deconcentration, in other words towards power dispersal, might be afoot in world affairs. The trend is not very

strong but concentration ratios have shown a steady decline from the level of about ninety six at the end of World War II to the low of about seventy six in 1972. Over the past quarter century therefore the significance or, to use an antitrust analogy, the share of the market attributable to the major power centres, may have declined by twenty points.

This review of military capacity therefore shows no evidence for multipolarity either at the present time or in the near future. Evidence points by contrast to unipolarity as characterising considerable periods and to a recent crystallisation of bipolarity with 'joint rule' as one of its possible variants. There is no comparably systematic evidence on legitimacy and consensus but it might be argued from impressionistic evidence that legitimised bipolarity as I would call it, is the product of only the last few years, consolidated only in 1972-3 by the Nixon-Brezhnev summit meetings and institutionalised in the SALT talks and in agreements on mutual consultation (that were not very well observed during the October War of 1973). Indeed the Cold War might have been a contest over the legitimacy of Soviet claim to such 'joint rule'.

If you take the total of world military power as 100 then in 1970 on the basis of one set of data, it was distributed as follows: United States 37 per cent; USSR 31 per cent; rest of the world 32 per cent. In other words very roughly in three equal portions, but with the USA and USSR being the two main power centres involved. That is one set of figures and there is no need to go into qualifying them, for instance by drawing out the implications of the energy crisis[4] or any other crisis that might happen along. Suffice to say, however, that there is insufficient evidence for saying that the contemporary system has suddenly become stable or that the *status quo* has been permanently frozen. Provisional figures for 1973, supplemented by data published by the London Institute for Strategic Studies[5] confirm this. (What I am now quoting is derived from a different source than the preceeding percentages and therefore strictly speaking noncomparable. I would not wish to draw too many conclusions from it). If reliance is placed on that most recent set of estimates the proportions for 1973 might be USA 32 per cent, USSR 36 per cent and the rest of the world 32 per cent – including Europe (about 11 or 12 per cent). This would suggest that in the space of the past few years the position of superiority held for most of the postwar period by the United States in the military field may have been reversed and this could be a fact of some considerable significance. Structural change is indeed afoot in the world system (even if its impact remains to be determined), but what we are sure to say is that multipolarity is nowhere in sight.

Oligopolistic Structures of World Order-Keeping

You may ask why we take so much trouble — or why I have taken so much trouble — establishing these military power ratios. The answer is that they give us important information, that they help us to perceive the structure of world politics as the *structure of an industry* and let me just say something to clarify the nature of the industry I have already referred to, not without a touch of verbal flourish, as the world order-keeping industry. This is the industry concerned with maintaining order in the global system. It has producers, and its producers are those political military organisations that regularly act and operate upon the global scene, the strategic missile and bomber forces in the posture of mutual deterrence, the naval task forces that sail the oceans and those strategic reserve forces that stand ready to fly off at an hour's notice to all destinations. Generally these are the forces of the major powers and the diplomatic and international organisations associated with them and their action and interaction shapes world politics. The producers also share a common technology derived from the need to achieve global reach for their forces and not to be outdistanced by rivals. The arms race is the expression of this technological competition. The consumers or clients of this industry are manifold and varied: the world's general population who are powerfully affected by its operations; the populations of the major powers who maintain these establishments; and the governments of nation-states the world over who frequently call on the help of these establishments. The services provided are, not unlike those of other industries, varied: they include global peace and security, well being and also hope, status and illusion. But they are most strikingly displayed in the panoply of manoeuvres and in the huge machines of

59

war on the ready and in motion at moments of great international crisis. The stream of armaments poured by both the superpowers at short notice into the Middle East in the fall of 1973 illustrates this industry in action — its good and its bad points. That is to say the world order-keeping industry consists not of countries but of a complex of relations among producers and clients and must be distinguished from two other separate but related systems, that can also be characterised as industries: the nation-states and the global economic regulatory services, those concerned for instance with money or with trade.

Let me say something very briefly about each of these. The nation-state system is analytically separable from the world order-keeping industry, dominated by the great powers, which I have just described, even if in practice it is closely identified with it. Of the major powers engaged in global order operations there are, as we have seen, only a very few. Of nation states there are many, as many as 140 at this time. Both are industries that are global in coverage but whereas the major powers operate and provide (or fail to provide) security primarily at the global level and regionally, in deterrence on the ocean and over long distances, nation-states are political establishments confined to closely defined national areas. Nation-states provide order at the national level of politics against territorial disturbance and boundary infringement.[6]

The second set of establishments separable from the basic industry of global order-keeping are those concerned with the global regulation of specific areas. Finance and trade may be taken as the most representative and most organised of these, but there are others. Whereas the world order complex is a sphere of foreign and defence ministers with some link, often weak, with the United Nations political structure, the money or trade tracks are the province of finance, trade and economic ministers, working also with their respective central banks and the world financial institutions, and forming notably strong networks of their own. One politically significant characteristic of this system is the absence from it to date of the Soviet Union and China in contrast to their strong position in the order system. The money, commercial and possibly also now the energy tracks have their own arrangements for governance and decision-making and while not unrelated to the global order track or the nation-states are distinct and notable for greater decentralisation. These

60

regulatory arrangements derive their functions from the large volume of transnational interactions that has been the characteristic of modern society but whose regulation has only recently emerged as a subject for formalised international action (the subject of transnational relations is the subject of the earlier lecture in this series by Professor J. Nye).

The separateness of the global order system from the nation-states and from the economic arrangements testifies to a significant degree of noncumulation in the world political structure. Those standing high in the great power system, for instance the USSR, need not rank high in the trade or financial regulatory networks and *vice versa*, those with much power in the international trade areas, for instance Japan, may have little to contribute to the order system of the power centres. The best governed nation-states, perhaps Switzerland or the Scandinavian countries, may have only marginal significance in world order questions and again, less than perfectly governed states may be high on the power pole. This would tend to show that specialisation of function has made some progress in the global system and that simple core-periphery models are not adequate for dealing with this complexity. This diversification of functions or functional differentiation may also extend to the web of multinational corporate activity as yet not very effectively surveyed by the regulatory system but developing some notions of distance from the power centres.

So much for the identity of the industry that we have been studying. Our interest in its structure resides in the belief that different structures have different consequences, that different structures produce different behaviour. In our early analysis the principal questions were related to the possible emergence of multipolarity and to the demonstrated interest of analysts in the differential impact of bipolar as against multipolar structures. A consensus as to what these differences might be is not evident. Some of the writers on the subject and in the literature have claimed for multipolarity the virtues of flexibility while others have lauded the certainty and the economy of bipolarity. Critics of these structures point on the other hand to the alleged competitiveness and war-proneness of the multipolar system, but also to the reputed rigidity and lack of responsiveness of bipolar arrangements. Empirical validation of these propositions has, however, been lacking. Given the non-obviousness of the question as to what makes a system multipolar, and also given the possible unreliability of data relevant to answering this and the variety of data that bears upon it, the establishment of an association between types of structure on the one hand and behavioural outcomes is far from simple. Nor has analysis paid sufficient attention to the fact that important periods and areas may in fact have been subject to unipolarity.

Upon reflection, therefore, there may not be much to choose between these rival associations, alleging either the virtues or the demerits of either multipolarity or bipolarity. The explanation would seem to be that both multipolarity and bipolarity are variants of one basic condition known to economists as oligopoly – a system characterised by the interaction of a very few but complex and powerful actors who communicate closely and are well informed of each others' activities, so that the strategy of each is likely to exert immediate effect on all the others. Theoretically, oligopoly is known to be indeterminate. The analysis of oligopoly centres on the problem of oligopoly rent which the producers are capable of extracting from the market; it shares this problem with monopoly. It is also concerned with the competitive-cooperative relationship that characterises the members of an oligopolistic industry. If this analogy is correct it would then follow that bipolarity would be as conflict-prone and competitive as multipolarity but would also be capable of producing periods of relative stability and that would be so because both bipolarity and multipolarity are variants of an oligopolistic system. To those who operate these industries it may matter whether two, three or five great firms share a market among themselves but to the public at large the difference may not be great.

A classic case of oligopoly is of course the automobile industry in the United States and indeed in the world; the computer industry is another example of oligopoly verging on monopoly. But the most striking recent example of international oligopoly has, for several decades past, been the oil industry. Oligopolies share a number of predictable characteristics that define their impact on society. They use large-scale production organisations, they rely on research and development to effect product innovations and on technology races to keep competitors off balance and market securely in control. They have strong marketing arrangements and resort to advertising and propaganda to differentiate their products, gain market power and induce consumer loyalty. The same characteristics are also shared by the world order-keeping industry, and let me spell out four of these that are relevant to this problem.

1. Oligopolistic industries collect a rent that is a return higher than one that could be obtained in a competitive industry, in conditions of perfect competition. The size of that rent for the world order industry is, of course, not easy to determine, but even a cursory look shows world order-keeping to be extremely powerful, prestige laden and far from effectively regulated. The industry currently absorbs in its operations at least 5 per cent of world product and this could be higher. In times of world war, at times of severe international crisis, its share has been known to rise to as high as one third of world product — as it did at the peak of World War II. One hundred years ago world order-keeping, on my estimates again, absorbed no more than one per cent of world product. This would seem to be some indicator of the size of rents that are accruing here. The result is a nonoptimal allocation of world resources and a diversion of immense proportions to non-priority purposes. But nonoptimality may also be the result of inefficiency, waste or just sheer laziness.

2. The size of the resources committed to this industry and the gains that may be realised within it provide an incentive for producers to cooperate for the maintenance and protection of this privileged status. A variety of forms of collusion among great powers serves to preserve the oligopolistic position of the industry, protect its position and consolidate its hold on customers by a division of markets as spheres of influence. The diplomatic system rests essentially upon the importance of common agreement not to rock the boat in the interest of the continuation of the *status quo*.

3. But oligopoly gains also attract attention, provoke competition and conflict, and draw new firms into the industry. Despite tremendous barriers to entry represented by huge investments in weapons, the burdens of research and development and the resistance of existing power holders, there are always some among the states whose internal organisation needs and perceived external opportunities make a bid for

global status a possibility especially at times of uncertainty and crisis. (The most recent claimant to great power status appears to be the Shah of Iran, who has cast doubts upon the prospects of Japan in the great power league and staked out a claim for Iran). The industry also suffers from instability due in part to the high economic growth rate of the world system as a whole, but due as well to the high rate of product change characteristic of it and evident in particular in the arms race. This is, of course, the only industry whose instability threatens world survival.

4. Because oligopolistic organisations are usually large their problems are also closely allied to the predicaments of all large-scale organisations. These are exemplified in the gigantic scale of the United States and Soviet political and military systems that are the most powerful and the most complex ever assembled. World wide in the scope of their operations, they keep all corners of the globe under close surveillance and nothing (not even a hole in the ground) escapes the unblinking gaze of their satellites. Resembling huge machines these organisations are exquisitely adapted to attain important but narrowly defined goals, but the well-advertised goals of the giant units may in fact be of limited significance for the good life and the ideal community. Hence large organisations create both internal and external difficulties. Their self-government leaves much to be desired, and tends greatly to rely on hierarchical authority. It is open to question whether any large-scale organisations are in fact compatible with democracy. As Andrei Sakharov, the spokesman for democratisation in the USSR put it in respect of the huge Soviet military-industrial complex[7]: 'Militarisation of the economy leaves a deep imprint on international and domestic policy. It leads to encroachment on democratic rights, the open conduct of public affairs, the rule of law; it constitutes a threat to peace.' In the United States, the problems of Watergate have been in part attributed to the intrusion of national security methods and concerns into the practice of domestic politics. For society as a whole, reliance upon excessively large organisations means loss of flexibility and of the capacity to adjust to change. The inability of the oil industry to cope with (yet ability to profit from) an energy crisis that was for some years recognised to be approaching, seems to be a glaring example of a

structural flaw that is also common to the world order-keeping industry, because in that industry too, failure pays.

Neither in its cooperative nor in its competitive phases nor in its large-scale organisation does an oligopolistic industry have a great deal to commend it. While possibly justifiable in certain situations, and economists specify certain cost conditions where oligopoly is thought to be justified, such an industry is also a drain on social energy and resources and, at worst, it is a threat to survival. The overpowering strength of its units puts it almost by definition beyond the control of regulatory activity. For who is to regulate the regulators? But there is one other minor consideration to be sure that is entirely relevant in the context of this theoretical discussion of international relations.

In economic theory oligopoly is regarded as a weak area. Unlike perfect competition it is beyond the range of thoroughgoing analysis and is subject, as mentioned, to indeterminacy. The interdependence of powerful actors well appraised of each others' strategies makes analysis and prediction quite difficult. Some students have concluded that this same kind of difficulty inheres in the study of world politics, so prominently dedicated to the analysis of oligopolistic arrangements.[8] We cannot have good theory in international relations, they argue, because the most characteristic activities arising there are beyond the discipline of theory and possibly also beyond intellectual grasp and social control. For students of the subject dedicated to its theoretical advancement it is therefore of interest, if for this reason alone, to consider structures of world politics more amenable to theoretical treatment. Let us now turn our attention to this possibility.

Prospects for a Free System

Along the axis of alternatives given by the number of units 'entitled to rule' or 'sharing a market', perfect competition or a free system occupies one extreme pole defined by the presence of many competing units each oriented to the system rather than each other and each by pursuing its own interests also serving the goals of society. Adam Smith may have identified a fundamental property of social arrangements when he coined the term 'invisible hand'; he brought to life what had been there all the time but was obscured by the apologists of Leviathans, the capacity of social systems for spontaneous self-adjustment and self-governance. He has also given strong reasons for believing that a society taking advantage of this capacity can function more effectively and more fairly than others burdened by excessive overheads.[9] But even if for large sectors of society the free market serves as a standard by which social arrangements might be evaluated, can it also serve as a standard for the judging of world order-keeping, so notably the province of giant organisations of immeasurable power?

We do not suppose that a free world order-keeping system requires the breaking up of existing large states into small units of equal size along the lines, for instance, of Henry II of France's 'Grand Design' for seventeenth century Europe.[10] There is no reason to think that in a free system all units must be small or equal in size. Competitive industries of low concentration are known to display inequality of firm size. The nation-state system in its present distribution might need adjustment and some will undoubtedly occur but it is unlikely to need fundamental changes in this particular respect.

But assuming some such adjustment and some consequent decline in the saliency of the nation-state system, the possibility of structural change in world order-keeping in the direction of deconcentration might be envisaged along two main lines: firstly, through the natural evolution of world society as the unfolding of an inherent logic of modernisation; and secondly, through deliberate contrivance and the purposeful alteration of political and social institutions.

The idea that peace is inevitable, that it is a natural consequence of social progress is at least as old as Immanuel Kant. It is a further refinement of this idea to argue that the general progress of modern society especially of those of its aspects that impinge on the organisation of political and societal institutions, and military power in particular, ultimately leads towards a dispersion of power. Take for instance the effects of scientific and technological progress.[11] In the natural progression of events, the first to benefit from scientific research and technological developments are the established centres that support most of this work. Thus the industrial revolution conferred great advantages upon the European powers and the development of nuclear weapons on those who first launched them, but in the long run at any rate, the scientific networks diffuse knowledge and the advantages that might derive from such instruments and weapons to many units throughout the system, thus become a dispersing and equalising factor. Hence it would accord with general experience of the diffusion of technology, that nuclear weapons would gradually become available to many states and not just to the great powers. Only through continued technological change and huge outlays on research and development, which are crucial features of oligopolistic industries, can the established centres expect to hold their advantage.

A generalised process of deconcentration just as much as a universal tendency towards concentration in large industrial enterprises,[12] military organisations or even in cities, might be a part of modernisation. The basic processes are the transportation and the information revolutions, both processes making reality of two of the essential preconditions of a free system — full mobility and adequate information. In the same vein, concern over such human rights as freedom of movement and migration, and for a free press and against obstacles to a free flow of information, can be seen not as sentimentalism but as a force to maintain indispensable conditions for a free world order.[13] Provision for education at all levels is another such precondition because it affords opportunity to take advantage of available information and avenues for mobility.

One other precondition favourable to a self-adjusting society is now also evident. The world is not equipped with a strong central government. The lack of such an overbearing authority fully accords with traditional conceptions of a free society. The United Nations has been developing and increasing its range of specialised functions but its weakness is a positive advantage in the eyes of those who regard relative governmental weakness as a desirable quality in society.

In some important respects it might therefore be argued that the societal and environmental context is favourable to deconcentration in world politics and toward a movement for a more dispersed power system. In such a free, that is dispersed, system, we would expect the weight of world political and military institutions to be reduced to a lower level (because they would lose their oligopoly rents); this would be the natural method of arms control. But the empirical evidence on the state of world power concentration is not very encouraging on this score. As previously noted, some decline in concentration ratios can be observed since 1945 but the extent of the decline is not precisely staggering and uncertainties in relation to data sources weaken the grounds for hope in this direction. Even less encouraging is evidence on truly long-term trends. Over the past 100 years the tendency has been toward, rather than away from, concentration and toward accenting the burdens of the structure of the great powers. Just as puzzling is the evidence for a long run tendency toward an increase in the cost of maintaining world order from one to over five per cent of a rising world product, when it is contrasted with a constant or possibly even declining quality of that order. In short, we might be having less order but paying more for it.

In the light of such evidence the hope for a *natural* progression towards a dispersal of concentrated power cannot be entertained without some considerable qualification. The expectation of inevitable peace by invisible hands might have to be supplemented by some measure of contrivance or by what students of utilitarianism have described as the 'artificial identification of interests'.[14] In the universal harmony of interests such progress might indeed be possible but must be brought about by *deliberate* action because of the recognition that a highly concentrated power structure is unlikely to be compatible with a harmonious society. What measures would be required to achieve a free system of world order-keeping?

There are three processes through which an oligopoly might deconcentrate and lose salience: de-emphasis, disaggregation and diversification. De-emphasis is a form of benign neglect and occurs when, in declining industries, organisational functions and the scale of operations are kept constant, while other sectors of society are allowed and encouraged to expand and gain strength. The relative weight of the industry then declines and its hold on society diminishes. This might be the least painful process for bringing about industrial reorganisation.

Disaggregation is a form of functional differentiation and occurs when organisations develop lines of activity that lend themselves to autonomous operation. Thus historically the police function began to be generally disaggregated from the general military function only just over one century ago. The global security function of the nuclear missile forces might in the future be separated from those of conventional forces in national armies.[15] Disaggregation is one way whereby large organisations are reduced in size. More drastic forms of break-up of such units have historically included anti-trust activities (including bans upon mergers and break-up of excessively large enterprises such as Standard Oil in 1911); inheritance laws impeding the concentration of property especially land; land reforms designed to eliminate concentrations of agrarian power, and the dissolution of empires or powerful states after military defeat, for instance at the end of World War I and II. Underlying disaggregation and break-up is the conviction that bigness *per se* is harmful to society and that it is particularly dangerous when conspiracy might be present. The same thought underlies deliberate schemes for arms control.

Illustrating the two processes of deconcentration just given is the experience of the transport industry, and of railways in particular, fundamentally transformed in the space of one century in part through a drastic but gradual decline of the role of railways in society and in part also through disaggregation of such functions as passenger from freight service and urban from long-distance transportation. Lastly, the structure of transportation was also changed through diversification by means of new entrants (such as automobiles or aircraft). The creation of alternative structures, new organisation and networks as supplements to and substitutes for existing great power arrangements thus opens up other possibilities of active deconcentration. Strengthening the world media and developing independent research organisations, for instance, might go some way towards making redundant large intelligence networks. A well functioning United Nations system substitute for diplomacy and peacekeeping operations may obviate armed intervention in internal affairs. New structures are also needed in the field of security and defence organisation. The more avenues for substitution the less vital become the functions of the great powers.

This train of thought can be put in an even stronger form: for unless substitute arrangements are in fact developed, unless a free system has some chance of taking roots, the world could plunge into disorder, especially if nuclear weapons were to be widely dispersed. A world of many units — of many autonomous units — which is a basic ingredient of a free system is not an automatic guarantee of order and unless it is well provided with arrangements giving attention to the common interest it will deteriorate into chaos.

In a spirit of intellectual curiosity and open enquiry I have thus reviewed some theoretical possibilities of reorganisation for the global order keeping industry. No claim has been advanced that such reorganisation is just around the corner, but students of international relations would be well advised to have at the ready criteria of some analytical power, whereby existing systems and developing tendencies can be evaluated much in the way in which, for instance, international trade analysts are always ready to fall back upon the principles of free trade.

In world politics there are a number of structures that we need to consider more carefully as alternatives to pure oligopoly. They might be mixed systems. There is also *limited* or *controlled* oligopoly, a system based upon a few, possibly even only two, power centres, but one that could evolve upon that basis a global party system intertwined with a substantial complex of global institutions; in other words, a world two party system or possible a world multiparty system. Another possibility worth exploring along this axis of structural alternatives is unipolarity but, again, *limited* or *controlled* unipolarity; I believe this to be a type of global political arrangement that has been more important in the past than students of world politics, fascinated by the diplomatic artifices and histrionic fireworks of the European balance of power system, have given it credit for. In particular, the world order system of the nineteenth century (what I would call the British system of world order) needs careful study with a view to eliciting whatever lessons it might still hold for the global arrangements of tomorrow. But the basic judgemental concept for world politics ultimately has to be a free political system that keeps the leviathan at bay and through artful adaptation gives free rein to the self-adjusting propensities of world society. This is not a recipe for universal democracy but at least a concept that embodies a vote of confidence in mankind's capacity for self-correction and self-governance.

References

1. See also George Modelski, *World Power Concentrations: Typology, Data, Explanatory Framework* (Morristown, New Jersey: General Learning Press, 1974).
2. Writers on American foreign policy have seized with zeal upon the few administration statements that have attempted to put its policy in a framework of a search for a 'pentagonal' (that is multipolar) world order [see e.g. James Chace, *A World Elsewhere: The New American Foreign Policy* (New York: Scribner's, 1973)]. Whether such conceptions have played a significant part in the making of policy is in fact open to question.
3. World military expenditures series of the Stockholm International Peace Research Institute (1948-72) and of the United States Arms Control and Disarmament Agency (1961-71).
4. For instance, the transfer of wealth to the oil producers through higher oil prices. Because of this, the Shah expects Iran to reach, in the space of one generation, a position among the five most highly developed and most powerful countries in the world (Interview in *Der Spiegel*, 7 January 1974, pp. 24-31).
5. *The Military Balance 1973-74* (London, 1973).
6. The two systems may be reinforcing each other, possibly because of the lack of clear boundaries between them, and both have grown greatly over the past 100 years.
7. In 'Postscript' to 'Memorandum to Leonid I. Brezhnev', *Survey* No. 84, Summer 1973, pp. 233-4.
8. Oran Young, 'The Perils of Odysseus: On Constructing Theories of International Relations', in *Theory and Policy in International Relations*, R. Tanter and R.H. Ullman, eds. (Princeton, N.J.: Princeton University Press, 1973), pp. 190-5.
9. A self-adjusting society is not necessarily a *laisser faire* society: self-adjustment occurs only in the presence of well-understood conditions relating in particular to information mobility, entry barriers, values, collusion and the existence of many units, conditions that are not always met. Nor does a free system preclude the production of public goods; in fact it requires for its operation that public goods producing the several conditions of self-adjustment (information, etc.) be made available by public if not by private means.
10. Known as one of the earliest schemes of international organisation, the Grand Design, as formulated by the Duke of Sully and also Elizabeth I of England,

was intended to divide Europe equally among fifteen states, in such a manner that 'none of them might be capable of giving umbrage to the rest'. A bold and famous plan, it was in fact a device for deconcentrating the Habsburg Empire: 'To confine the power of the House of Austria

w   within just bonds'. *Memoirs of Maximilian de Bethune, Duke of Sully* . . . (3rd ed., London, 1761), Vol. II, pp. 72-3, Vol. III, p. 343.

11. The growth of technology is sometimes thought to lead inexorably toward concentration. A concise statement of how technology might be seen to strengthen free competition is Walter Eucken, 'Technik, Concentration und Ordnung der Wirtschaft', *Ordo,* 1950, Vol. III, 3-17.

12. A law of concentration is an important tenet of Marxist thought. An early statement may be found in Friedrich Engels' 'Conclusion' to the *'Critique of Political Economy'* (1844).

13. They are the preconditions for the operation of exit and voice as mechanisms for maintaining organisational performance. A.O. Hirschman, *Exit, Voice and Loyalty: Responses to Decline in Firms, Organizations and States* (Cambridge, Mass.: Harvard University Press, 1970). They also serve as mechanisms of deconcentration in that they make it possible to reduce, and change the size and scope of, such organisations.

14. Elie Halevy, *The Growth of Philosophic Radicalism* (London: Faber and Faber, 1928), p. 17.

15. For a fuller statement see George Modelski, *Principles of World Politics* (New York: The Free Press, 1972), pp. 299-304.

4 AN INTERNATIONAL 'SCIENTIFIC SOCIETY'?

E.B. Haas

We often hear the term 'scientific society' used as a description of the society in which we live. Moreover, common usage imbues the term with a dark prophecy concerning our destiny: since there are so many things wrong with science, a society dominated by it is certain to come to a bad end. The same common usage, however, also holds out a friendlier prognosis which suggests that if there are things wrong with science, they can also be fixed by science itself and thus make our future both more scientific and more benign. You may well wonder why, if the term is so ambiguous as to induce optimism and pessimism at the same time, I would wish to extend its meaning into the international arena to which it has not yet been applied.

Before responding, I offer a definition of what the term means to me. A society can be considered 'scientific' if three key attributes are in fact found in it: public issues are dominated by scientific and technological concerns; persons and institutions concerned with defining and solving problems which arise in society are informed by cognitive maps which incorporate scientific concepts and techniques; these persons and their institutions are largely scientific-technological experts in terms of their skills and roles. The dominance of public issues by considerations of science and technology is not hard to demonstrate in most industrialised countries. Concern with the performance of the economy, the defence system, training and education, housing and urban development, transporation and mental health — these are the mainstays of public policy. It is less obvious that the managerial concepts used for attacking these problems are also imbued with science; some are more so than others. However, to the extent that the techniques of systems analysis and forecasting are increasingly employed over the entire range of public policy choice, the scientific thrust becomes dominant particularly if used by economists, lawyers and social workers, rather than only by engineers, medical doctors, city planners and specialists in administration. Finally, it is probably not accurate to argue that our society is already ruled by the technostructure of experts skilled in these occult arts. On the other hand, the weight of these arcana is certainly felt in public life. While it is not true that the business executive and the corporation lawyer, the professional politician and the professional military man have been overshadowed by scientifically and technologically trained personnel, it is true that an ever more complex symbiosis between these skills and roles is manifest. None of our societies is fully scientific in the sense of my definition; some, however, are getting pretty close. And when a dozen societies of the industrial northern hemisphere get there at more or less the same time, something we might call an international scientific society will be born.

Now what is wrong with such a development? There are technetronic celebrations and countercultural denunciations. I believe that the weighty role of science and technology is inevitable because most of us refuse to do without the more obvious benefits. But I do not agree entirely with the main reasons given by those who see nothing wrong with the birth of an international scientific society. They see technology as associated with progress, with emancipation from invalid or frag- mentary knowledge, from superstition, from subjectivism, from ideology. The scientific society not only improves the lot of mankind because the mastery of nature facilitates higher levels of physical welfare, but also because the scientific rationality offers the hope of a problem-solving epistemology superior to mankind's traditional ways of making collective choices. Whatever may be wrong with science, these voices say, systematic planning will cure it, while the subordination of science to political and social priorities will kill it.

Critics of this view are not hard to find. I shall exclude the neo-luddite variety of attack and that of the ecofreak because these critics are in revolt not merely against the instrumental rationality specific to science but against all types of rational control. Among the remaining 'antiscientists' the main lines of criticism are two: (1) scientific knowledge is probably superior to other kinds of knowledge, but it is invariably misused when applied to public decision-making; and (2) scientific knowledge, even if it were not misused, is dangerously flawed and therefore should not be blandly incorporated into the making of public decisions. Each line of argument deserves more attention.

Those who claim that scientific knowledge is usually misused when applied to policy-making point out that experts advising the government are usually interested only in acting as a pressure group in support of their research interests; that officials seeking expert advice are interested largely in finding legitimacy for decisions already made on nonscientific grounds; that experts and officials, even if acting without such motives, tend to subordinate their technical knowledge to serving the wrong values, such as increasing the GNP, training more technical manpower, or bolstering their country's international prestige. And even if there were no self-serving motivations and misguided values in the picture, the institutional imperfections of government are such that scientific knowledge does not find its proper and dominating role for reasons having to do with the nonfunctioning of advisory committees and panels.

Those who doubt the virtues of science as a superior kind of knowledge advance quite different arguments in articulating the malaise without, however, arriving at the conclusion that a more 'Scientific Society' is either impossible or undesirable. Science is too fragmented and specific to allow sufficient substantive agreement for scientific experts to appear as the new philosopher kings; scientists do not know enough about the links among natural systems to make sweeping knowledge claims. More important, the scientific method is a very imperfect tool and hence should not be accepted uncritically as a superior problem-solving epistemology. Why is this said to be so? Because the 'classical' scientific method actually operates only under very exceptional circumstances, and the conditions under which R & D is in fact done today all but guarantee that these circumstances will not be replicated. Runaway technology and industrialised science militate against the proper use of the classical method. In addition, scientific experts tend to subordinate the advice they give, ostensibly on technical grounds, to their personal ideological preferences. And even if this were not so, the institutional network within which scientific research is encouraged and funded is such as to work against the application of the classical methodology because the social goals of scientists are enmeshed with the political and economic goals of the governments to such an extent as to make science the handmaiden of politics. But the most telling argument is the conviction that the scientific epistemology, even if it were not flawed along these lines, is specific to the investigation of nature and cannot be easily applied to the study of man and society; hence it is not a tool which should be used for policy making. Some argue that even if the epistemology could be applied, methodological constraints remain sufficiently weighty to insulate the knowledge-producing process from the context in which the knowledge is to be put to work for the public good. But the fact remains that even these critics concede that something more 'scientific' has to be done about relating the unintended and hitherto unforeseen consequences of science and technology to the future of society.

If these are faults of national scientific societies, they could hardly be banished from its international counterpart. What are the remedies currently being debated? Incremental institutional reforms are suggested by those who merely see a misuse of scientific knowledge. If scientists take their duties as critics seriously, they need not be in despair over their alleged inability to rationalise politics in the long run. In fact, they often claim that science gives them the knowledge base to better influence society, as by the Federation of American Scientists and the Pugwash Movement.

It is to this line of attack that we owe such innovations as technology assessment, environmental impact studies, offices of science and technology, simulation and gaming in the anticipation of consequences likely to result from the introduction of new technologies, systematic forecasting, Delphi studies and the like. Moreover, the techniques of adversary science and technology, deliberately pitting expert against expert, are an outgrowth of this line of thought. While the practice has surfaced, its practitioners would like the process to become institutionalised and legitimated through appropriate reforms in the governmental system of advisory panels and committees, research centres, and the practice of public interest law.

Critics who question the character of scientific procedure and knowledge itself are not satisfied with these solutions. Their remedies are more sweeping. We shall label them 'designers of change' and 'evolutionary systems thinkers'.

Designers of change believe that they can specify the kinds of changes society needs and ought to need. They consider it possible and desirable to design the kinds of institutions able to accomplish such changes. They also consider it desirable to recognise the permanence of the scientific society and hence wish to design the kinds of institutions which will continue to change without needing to be redesigned as new demands and technological possibilities arise. The approach proceeds on the assumption that 'if we want to maximise such-and-such a value, and if technology promises such-and-such a breakthrough, then we ought to have such-and-such a set of social arrangements'. The implication is, of course, that the proper kind of scientific knowledge (not, perhaps, the knowledge which is now purveyed) is capable of giving us this improved method of making rational choices.

Evolutionary systems thinkers tend to be critical of premature claims made by certain '*laisser innover*' scientists about the automatic liberating qualities of scientific knowledge; but they, in turn, claim to be on to a new type of more comprehensive understanding which may make Cordorcet a proper prophet in the longer run. The following instances come to mind: comprehensive ecological systems which link what is known of various natural systems and which contain guidelines for action on such questions as food resources, energy resources, the purity of air and water and therefore the 'quality of life'; cybernetic systems which purport to tell us how much information we can store, use, and correct, and then re-use for better decisions; evolutionary systems claiming to understand the interface between biological evolution and social adaptation, particularly as being advocated by some geneticists and molecular biologists. For such approaches, better science is the key to redesigning society and government; indeed, it is the only guarantee of human survival in the face of the misuse and the misunderstanding to which science has already been put.

What does all this have to do with international relations? In an age of decolonisation, it hardly requires emphasis that the previous five hundred years of imperial expansion of Europe — and the international system which arose as a result — was due largely to the unequal development and diffusion of technological skills and capabilities. The benefits of science and scientific thinking accurately foretold by Bacon came to be the political and military property of Western states. In short, the evolution of national scientific societies at unequal rates creates specific patterns, blocs and institutions of international life. The desire for emulation then sets in. Regions, nations and groups who consider themselves disadvantaged now begin crash programmes of acquiring the same capabilities, sometimes for cultural, more often for economic and military reasons. The structure of international life is altered to the extent that the newcomers are successful. Today their efforts are aided by international programmes of deliberate technology diffusion, technical education and planned industrialisation. To that extent, then, international organisations and national policy have become agents for the universalisation of science and technology.

That much is obvious. For the most part, this effort has taken the *'laisser innover'* form of development; science and technology — internationally — have been considered forces for progress, liberation, equality and dignity. Already, however, the concern with unwanted consequences of technology first manifest in the older industrialised countries has made its appearance on the international scene as we witness the first programmes, not for creating new technological capabilities only, but to control by common means the unwanted consequences of technology. Both at the global and regional levels, then, programmes of environmental protection and improvement of the quality of life have begun to reflect the desire for making science safe for society. The institutional implications of these developments are now visible in the huge international network of scientific expert panels, the joint research programmes of the International Council of Scientific Unions, the growth of international laboratories, international registries of noxious substances, nuclear energy safeguards and coordinated antipollution measures.

If that were all, we might well conclude that the net impact of the spreading of technological skills beyond national boundaries is confined to increasing and diffusing *national* capabilities, as well as the growth of international institutions adequate to make it safe for nations to exploit these capabilities. Instead of a truly 'international' scientific society, such a trend would merely give us an international system made up of varyingly complex patterns of competing and cooperative national scientific societies. The primacy of the sovereign state might be enhanced rather than undermined, as the state helped by scientists becomes the main agent for making science safe for society. On balance, I would say that this is what *has* happened so far.

But what if the fears and prophecies implicit in the criticisms of the national scientific society were to become an international phenomenon? What if the organs of the UN Environmental Program, of UNESCO, of FAO, of IAEA, of the UN Committee on Outer Space were to become agents of incremental reform in the functioning of scientific rationality? What if technology assessment were to become an international function, or the forecasting of technological trends and their possible impact on trade, employment, urbanisation? What if the practices of adversary science were to become part of international institutional and normative processes?

I now offer three scenarios of an international scientific society based on the critical views of science described before. The impetus for the three is the same: an effort to make science and technology safe for mankind while also guarding against the abuses, misunderstandings and misapplications of science which are the core of the current malaise. Each of the three is articulated, in general terms, in the current literature.

Incremental reform in national scientific societies — which are considered 'good' on balance — is the theme of the celebrated OECD report of which Harvey Brooks was the main author. The report recommends that pure scientific research be left strong and autonomous from social guidance but that the technological applications of such research to industry be made part and parcel of a more systematic approach to industrial development, economic control, education and the safeguarding of the quality of life. The scientific method — in the form of data banks, formal models of large systems and the use of social indicators — is to be featured in socialising science. Social science itself is to become part of the ensemble, instead of the stepchild it now is. Orderly development of societies too complex to rely on market mechanisms and incentives is the aim. International research and forecasting for arriving at the proper indicators, data and projections is the method. If acted upon, the report would effectively subordinate national investment in R & D, secondary and higher education, social welfare, foreign aid and setting of policy priorities in this field, to an international technocracy of experts whose work and advice would suffice to harmonise and coordinate the policies of the constituent nations. Technology assessment and guidance would be internationalised.

Sweeping reform is the objective of the Club of Rome, our instance of a would-be designer of change. Minor institutional tinkering is considered inadequate to stave off the converging crises in resources, energy, pollution, urbanisation and food which confront the world. Large-scale redesign of economic and social practices is called for to save the world. This involves a major reconceptualisation of the relationships and feedbacks between natural and social systems to emphasise the reality of 'limits to growth' and the place of human arrangements in the natural order. It also involves a thoroughgoing revaluation of western norms toward an acceptance of nature instead of the desire to master and rape her. And all this calls for major changes in how man makes collective decisions – in other words, in national and international government. While no blueprints for a new world order are included in the Club of Rome's scenario, we can extrapolate the need for a world central planning mechanism to which almost all aspects of the national scientific society's activities would be subjected. Institutionally as well as normatively, the change to be designed involves world government and a world religion based on an appreciation of the promise and the limits of science. The old Platonic Academy becomes the World Academy of Sciences of the future.

Is this vision too fanciful to serve as a guide to a possible world order? How many global energy crises, famines, nuclear accidents, radioactive weather systems, competitive satellite observations, extermination of fish populations due to marine pollution, monetary chain reactions or unprecedented mass unemployment situations would it take to make the scenario credible? Even if no single scientific-religious priesthood with its Master Model emerges, it is not fanciful to imagine the rapid evolution of a series of regimes and organisations with responsibility for sectors and aspects of the 'total crisis'. While this would still be incrementalism, it would go some way toward universalising concerns and regulatory patterns, projections and plans which are now the sole property of national governments and of multinational corporations. The visions of evolutionary systems thinkers are not inconsistent with the views of the designers of change, but they carry the argument a step farther. The issue is not only the danger of self-destruction of national scientific societies because of their neglect for the links and chains among imperfectly understood natural and social phenomena. The issue is also the genetic and cultural future of human society as a whole. Evolutionary systems thinkers believe in the perfectibility of man, in influencing his evolution toward a 'higher' kind of species, in the 'ethisizing' function of biological evolution, as C.H. Waddington put it. Some anthropologists consider the evolution of social arrangements of an increasingly cooperative type the 'evidence' for this mode of adaptation. And Teilhard de Chardin combined the biological and anthropological perspectives with a theology of postulating the continuity between physical and cultural evolution as ending in a spiritual communion with God, a communion applicable to all mankind and not just to the individual. There is, to be sure, considerable disagreement as to whether this course of events can be accelerated by controlling culture and permitting biology to produce appropriate genetic results, or to reverse the procedure by redesigning cultural patterns in order to permit scientists to manipulate genetics so as to produce a better man. In both cases, however, there is a clear connection between the scientific understanding of large-scale systems and the desire to manipulate them for social and religious reasons. The implications for government, while hardly clear, are nevertheless quite staggering.

It is more difficult to imagine scientific and technological crises which would trigger such control processes than in the previous scenario. However, new breakthroughs in genetics, biomedical engineering and public health practices may make my scepticism obsolete very soon. In any event, imagine the kind of planning required to make society safe for evolution, or evolution safe for society. Not only would geneticists and molecular biologists become kings; what is more disturbing to me is that sociologists and anthropologists would become their prime ministers. And on the international scene, the prophetic role imagined by Julian Huxley for UNESCO in 1946 would become stark reality.

My point is this: the very anxieties engendered by the nature and impact of science at the national level, when transferred to international relations, *could* be the most powerful trigger for large-scale structural change in world relations. The international scientific society, in addition to being the agent of the universalisation of technology, could also become the instrument for changing what we have thus far called international politics because of the very fears aroused by that universalisation.

And this brings me to the real purpose which may be served by the concept of an international scientific society. One could talk about such a society as a symbol — more or less rhetorically — of the good in store for the underdeveloped countries and perhaps for the industrial world. One could also use it as a phrase to conjure up all the evil which awaits us globally if we wish to identify with the ecology movement. Some of the current commentators — Lester Brown, Richard Falk, the Sprouts, Victor Ferkiss — do just that. This is not my purpose. I am concerned with elaborating the notion as an ideal type for imagining the trends, hopes, fears and learning patterns emerging from the mixture of capabilities and aspirations so as to see how they combine, mingle, mix and separate. If it is too much to claim that such an ideal type gives us a purchase on a *single* new world order, it is probably safe to imagine several alternative orders which may well coexist temporally and spatially and yet result in a net change in the international system. I present some currently visible clues along these lines.

There is already strong evidence that late developing countries view science and technology as social artifacts which can be bent and used to advance social evolution, a view encouraged by western scientists who advise them and the United Nations bodies which finance appropriate assistance. At the moment this conviction does not go beyond the desire to catch up with what they perceive the West to have attained. But need matters stop at that point? If the West adopts 'no growth' policies and Latin America and Asia decide to forge ahead with the creation of more scientific societies at home, the mismatch in eventual capabilities is likely to trigger a global military crisis. Such a setting is conducive to notions of an international scientific society dedicated to the collective and progressive evolution of all. Again, science and technology themselves would then serve as the trigger and the cognitive maps for adjusting the world to science and technology.

The scenario of the Brooks Report is not fanciful at all. The other two do strain our credulity quite a bit more. But we ought to remind ourselves that the experience of the past is no longer an adequate guide for disciplined speculation about world order. Even the acceptance of the least strained of the scientific-technological scenarios undeniably suggests the obsolescence of the sovereign state, if not in law then in fact. If we accept the notion that it is no longer possible to plan national R & D policies — and hence the rhythm of economic growth, employment, education and social stratification — simply because too many of the crucial variables entering into R & D planning escape national control, then we are automatically forced to consent to some measure of *non-national* harmonisation, coordination or joint action. No single actor can even suboptimise meaningfully without the cooperation of all other crucial actors, let alone optimise. To satisfice across such a range of interconnected issues simply leaves no alternative to joint action once it becomes apparent that the minimum common denominator of the past — a relatively free market for science, technology and industry — is no longer tolerable. On the other hand, the opposite of the free market — central planning of the ensemble by the sovereign state — does not appear possible even for satisficing purposes for any nation other than a successful totalitarianism.

Joint action, however, need not mean world government, regional federation, supranationalism of the European Community variety, or any of the familiar legal and constitutional formulas. It may even imply the greater participation of subnational political units. The variety of arrangements already existing and imaginable quite exceeds any of the established forms. The sovereign state, though it still acts as if it were the hegemon, is simply pretending to mastery of events. But there is no obvious successor in sight to take its place. I see no need to imagine a single successor, or a single *type* of successor.

83

Our designers of change have a field day with international life because they conclude that national planning is no longer very effective. The conditions of interdependence — in terms of the interaction of capabilities — would then act as the trigger for massive international plans of designed change which would bring the abuses of the scientific mode under control once more. Evolutionary systems thinkers with their emphasis on the survival of whole systems and the stimulation of negative entropy flows would turn to international politics as 'the system' which most closely corresponds to the ecological wholeness which is to be safeguarded.

The notion of the international scientific society is therefore a mind stretcher which permits us to imagine within some credible constraints how alternative arrangements, comprehensive or piecemeal, may come into being. It also permits us to speculate, with less discipline, how experience with such arrangements may have the effect of inducing new expectations and thus permit us to learn how to combine the larger vision, that comes from scientific techniques of analysis, and use it in government policy making. The adoption of such a stance does not tell us and cannot tell us which arrangement is best, which is to be desired. It can inform us of the fuller scope of the causes of our malaise, not the final and definitive scope. It can suggest how food and energy needs interact, not whether food is more important than energy. It can show how the uses of the ocean compete and make optimal utilisation of any one ocean resource feasible. It cannot tell us which of various rival uses should be favoured. It can give us comparative statistics on the quality of life, not determine whether crowding is a greater evil than noise.

It is incorrect to say that the evolution of alternative world orders is a function of values and not technology. It is equally incorrect to argue the opposite. Alternative world orders will develop from the *interaction* between scientific knowledge — the constraint — and new social purposes — the goal. The alternatives to the sovereign state remain to be worked out in this interaction. There is little reason to suppose that any single alternative will either be devised or found acceptable. There is every reason to imagine that our increasing use of science and technology, to benefit from them and to control their unwanted effects, will also inform the range of options we devise for making the world livable. Science will teach us about the chains of physical and social interdependence within which we are increasingly enmeshed. Human purposes will tell us how we will use this knowledge in the construction of alternatives.

These purposes can range from maximising the efficient use of double-bottomed tankers to the creation of a global ecosystemic theocracy. They may include the diffusion of technological skills for their own sake, to the subordination of technology to comprehensive economic or social development, no matter under whose ideological auspices. In short, what we do with our increased understanding of the natural and social world is in large measure determined by the kind of society we wish to maintain or create. But our understanding of what is possible and desirable remains partly determined by our changing understanding of what we believe to be true of nature and man. That understanding is a product of science. Modern man is not free to bend his instrumental knowledge to his political will because his political will is increasingly fashioned by his instrumental knowledge.

By positing this interaction, I am able to eliminate from relevance some political forms without being able to specify with even remote probability the shape of their successors. I think I know what will not be, but I cannot tell what there will be – except to suspect that it will not be the product of pure political will. The international 'scientific society', then, is a construct designed to enable us to reason about our collective future by taking as given that man has never been the same since Galileo and Bacon and never will be. But it is also a construct designed to warn us that scientific knowledge can be abused and misused by the state and to suggest how safeguards against abuse, in turn, can lead to alternatives to the state.

5 ELITE PERCEPTIONS AND THEORIES OF WORLD POLITICS

Bruce M. Russett

Why Perceptions Matter

'International politics' have changed greatly in recent years. But precisely how? Faced with the evidence of change in many spheres, we can easily ignore continuing aspects of stability, or fail to take appropriate measure of the depth and consequences of change. Consider, for example, three distinct elements of interest: the basic *structure* of international power relationships; the *behaviour* of national governments toward one another and toward various non-national groups within or transcending nation-states; and the *perceptions* of politically influential figures about the structure and behaviour of world politics. Changes in each of these elements need not be of the same degree nor have the same timing.

The policy orientation and behaviour of the major national governments has changed fairly dramatically over the past decade. Limited *détente* between the United States and the Soviet Union, and the United States and China; a general relaxation of the Cold War and avoidance of overt military threats between East and West; modest achievements in arms control; the intensified, protracted hostility between the Soviet Union and China, once closely allied; increasingly independent behaviour by the major European states: all these are well-recognised. Indeed most people's perceptions of world politics have changed even more drastically. Consider the wide-spread expectations of continuing and deepened *détente* and peaceful coexistence; the nearly complete erosion of fears of a communist invasion into Western Europe; the rise and broad acceptance of more or less revisionist histories about the origins of the Cold War; recognition of new power centres in China, Japan and Western Europe; acknowledgement of the decay of American military supremacy; the American turning away from the so-called 'responsibilities of world power' to a posture typified by a limited degree of political 'isolationism'; coupled with a general belief in the economic and physical interdependence of the globe which demands concerted action to preserve the earth from the consequences of pollution, resource depletion and overpopulation — problems hardly considered in the early 1960s. In short, the perceptions of most persons concerned with world politics have changed at a faster rate, and at more nearly discontinuous jumps, than has the behaviour of governments. With those changes in perceptions have come equally significant changes in preferences.

Equally important, however, is the contrast they make to the much more modest changes that have occurred in international power relationships, the underlying structure of much of international politics. Indeed, the reality of some of these structural conditions belies the widespread perceptions of great change. Professor Modelski's paper in this volume is a good statement of how limited these changes among the major powers have been. Whether one looks at an index of immediate military capability, or of moderate term national strength such as gross national product or energy consumption, the picture is essentially the same. American predominance over the Soviet Union has narrowed somewhat since the 1950s, but the superpowers' superiority over the number three and smaller powers remains without major alteration. China and Japan have moved up, and Britain down, but the gap to superpower status for either is still very large despite Japanese economic growth and Chinese accession to the ranks of thermonuclear powers. Nor did either the Chinese or the Japanese accomplishments take place overnight. Public recognition came rather suddenly, but whatever change in status has occurred took place gradually over two decades.

There are of course real limits to the purposes for which military or economic power bases are relevant, and even the power relations should be modified for the waxing and waning of alliance links among the major states, such as increased European integration. The meaning of the figures is nonetheless indisputable: the structure of international power relationships has *not* changed greatly since early in the Cold War period. Our perceptions have changed greatly, and often appropriately so. But they deceive us if they lead us to imagine a change in power relationships that has not really occurred.[1]

Most emphatically, this is not to say that because power relationships have not changed much since the Cold War we should return to the perceptions and attitudes of the Cold War era. If our perceptions are currently out of step with reality in any noteworthy degree, they probably were equally so during the Cold War. Then the bipolar structure of world politics, and especially the magnitude of the 'Soviet threat', were almost surely exaggerated, and it would not help to reincarnate previous error. Furthermore, there have been important behaviour changes by the major powers, affecting a variety of policies, that profoundly modify the *effect* of the power relationships. The point is simply that behaviour has changed notably, probably less than have perceptions but more than power relationships. How is it, then, that what we formerly perceived as an appropriate set of policies neither is nor is perceived to be appropriate any longer? Why have policy and especially perceptions changed so much? Can we identify current perceptions much more precisely, with some better evidence on the details, timing and causation of the changes? And what will be the feedback effect of changed perceptions on policy? Certainly there will be major effects. After all, 'objective' conditions in the 'real world' must always be filtered through our perceptual lenses; it is what we see, not what 'is', that affects our response.

It is important, therefore, to look carefully at whatever evidence is available about elites' preferences and perceptions about international politics. Using the word 'elite' in this context does not imply any acceptance of 'power elite' theories or of any ideas about interlocking interests or even conspiracies directing the government. We simply use it in a manner perhaps roughly comparable to 'leaders' or prominent individuals. We mean first those people involved at high levels in the political process, such as party politicians and officials, senior civil servants, leaders in the mass media and leaders of interest groups involved in political activities. Along with them we include high level executives of major corporations and labour unions, and more generally the sort of professional and upper status people who we know are especially likely to vote, to take an interest in international affairs, to make campaign contributions and to lobby. We thus are identifying the sorts of people especially relevant to political decision-making, but we are making no prior assumptions that particular individuals or types of people are heavily involved in particular decisions or that they can in any way be identified as sharing particular interests or preferences. It will be convenient to focus on the United States, but that also serves as an opportunity to develop some ideas that may be of more general interest.

We want to know these people's policy preferences and perceptions regarding foreign political and military activities, what they see as the proper role of the United States in the contemporary world. It will be useful to focus on attitudes on national security questions, and especially attitudes toward the Vietnam experience and future military and political involvements of the United States in the world and particularly in the less developed countries. We want to understand what was the attitudinal basis for what is variously termed the 'internationalist' or 'activist' or 'interventionist' policy of the United States in the post-World War II era, and how and to what degree that basis has changed. That understanding is important in reaching any expectations for future world order, and for any action designed to influence the shape of that order. We start, then, with a policy problem and a need for information, which in turn demands theoretical explanation.

Theoretical Overkill

Theories about what drives or has driven American foreign policy are much in evidence. American foreign policy has, in terms of its expressed aims, achieved a mixture of success and failure over the past thirty years. Perhaps the successes have, on balance of quantity and importance, exceeded the failures. Nevertheless, one vibrant failure stands out to colour the view of almost everyone — Vietnam. Just as there are lots of theories about the sources of American foreign policy generally, there are lots of attempts to apply those theories specifically to the Vietnam

89

case, because that case has had such important consequences for America and the world, and primarily because the experience was so searing for Americans. It represents a puzzle that demands understanding.

The puzzle stems from the obvious failure of American policy in Vietnam, even in terms of the goals officially declared for that policy.[2] Variously described as for defending the Vietnamese, halting the spread of communism, or establishing the credibility of the American security guarantee for small countries, it effectively did none of those. The war virtually destroyed the society and culture of those it was supposed to defend. While as of this date a non-communist government remains in Saigon, its tenure of office looks extremely insecure, and that of the non-communist governments in Laos and Cambodia still more so. The credibility of the United States guarantee to defend small allies has been drastically weakened, not reaffirmed, by the effect of the Vietnam war on that country and on the United States itself. Given the death and devastation in that unhappy Asian country, few peoples or governments would now choose to be defended in similar manner. Although costs to America were in every way less severe than to Vietnam, they were bad enough: lives; money; social and political disruption of a degree virtually unprecedented over a hundred years. Thus quite on its own terms, even without challenging the essential wisdom or morality of those terms, the war was an utter failure.

It was a failure, moreover, in the opinion of most Americans. As early as 1967 and 1968 this was apparent to a majority. By October 1967 only 42 per cent in a Gallup Poll denied that 'the United States made a mistake sending troops to fight in Vietnam'.[3] The failure became apparent to the majority of careful observers, not to mention the populace in general, long before it was abandoned in 1973. Yet the American government, with its vast apparatus for intelligence gathering and evaluation, 'must' surely have been aware of the failure at least as soon as was the populace at large. Why then did it take so long before a decision to get out was finally taken and implemented? Four, or perhaps four and a half, different kinds of theories attempting to explain this can be singled out. We term them respectively 'strategic', 'bureaucratic', 'economic' and 'ideological' (the last with a subset of 'democratic') theories. There are still others, but these are the most prominent and will suffice to make our point.[4]

The first is the set of *strategic* theories, attributing the actions of American policymakers to their perceptions of security requirements and *realpolitik*. By this explanation, policy makers think in terms of military security, balance of power, containing Soviet and/or Chinese expansion, containing power centres in general, the importance of honouring commitments to defend one's military allies. This perceived need to match, contain, or repress rival world power centres stemmed in part from, or at least was reinforced by, the experiences of Britain, France and the United States in World War II. The Munich analogy was frequently drawn, as were explicit allusions to the failure to resist Japanese aggression in the 1930s.[5] In some versions the balance of power is always seen to be precarious, and a secure 'balance' really is considered to rest only on American predominance. In any case, by this line of thought the communist aspects of the post-World War II opponents are themselves of secondary importance.[6] Communism is incidental except as it is thought to add to the expansionist impulse, capability or attractiveness of the opponent. Policy makers holding strategically-oriented views basically are concerned with containing *any* rival power centre, regardless of its ideology or form of domestic organisation.

Bureaucratic theories are quite different. Strategic theories postulate the widespread existence of images of the *national* interest as expressed in power or security terms, where policy makers make decisions that are rational at least as defined by their conceptions of security needs and threats. Bureaucratic theories rather emphasise the competing interests of many rival individuals and agencies within the vast policy making organisations, with each caught up in pursuing its own interests or, at best, its own parochial view of the national interest where that national interest conveniently happens largely to coincide with the narrow bureaucratic interest. Organisations and governmental institutions thus get caught up in bureaucratic politics, with each agency or branch chief seeking to aggrandise or at a minimum protect the status of his agency and the continuation of agency policy.

To this end bureaucrats control information and intelligence passing up through the agency hierarchy, try to make the agency look good and to persuade their superiors that current policy as they are executing it is succeeding and should be maintained. As a result, policy makers at the very pinnacle may really be among the latecomers in getting accurate information on what is going on. Dependent on subordinates for intelligence, the top may become aware of a failure only after it has become widely manifest, even to the general public who do not derive their information so totally from the governmental bureaucracy as some political leaders may allow themselves to do. Under these circumstances the easy assumption that decision-makers must have known early about the Vietnam failure needs to be questioned. Public scepticism and disapproval might well lead rather than follow the man at the top. This would be especially true if the political leadership tended to give special weight to information from particular sources on the ground that it generally seemed 'harder' or better data-based than others. Allegedly this happened with the military information on Vietnam, where some 'softer' more pessimistic political estimates were ignored in favour of the deceptively solid and fully as self-serving estimates from the military.

Bureaucratic theories are concerned with difficulties in coordinating policy execution as well as with information processing. Just as agency chiefs and their subordinates may distort information, they may ignore or bend their superior's orders so as not to conflict with their own purposes. They may continue to pursue their own policies, or even take independent and unauthorised initiatives. The famous incident over American missiles in Turkey during the Cuban missiles crisis is a good example of the former. Premier Khrushchev intimated he might dismantl the Soviet missile bases in Cuba if the Americans did likewise with theirs in Turkey. President Kennedy's response was one of surprise and anger with his own military and political subordinates. He had in fact ordered the American missiles to be taken out of Turkey months before; by the time of the Cuban crisis he was not pleased to have them available as a *quid pro quo* for Khrushchev to demand. The general problem is simply that against determined bureaucratic interests with their own priorities and preferences, a chief executive can effectively change policy only by repeated and forceful intervention. There are severe limits to the number of times and places he can make such intervention, especially if he is also to maintain the morale and general loyalty of members of the bureaucracy. The larger the bureaucracy — and the United States defence and foreign policy bureaucracy is certainly large — the more severe these problems are likely to be.[7]

In trying to explain the Vietnam *embroglio* various observers have noted cases of biased intelligence and deliberate 'ignorance' or disregard of unwelcome orders within military and civilian agencies, bureaucratic infighting between agencies, and excessive zeal in continuing discredited policies by advocates of the Green Berets or 'pacification'. Military activities during the lost tacit bargaining period before the Paris peace talks have come in for special attention, including the choice and timing of bombing raids. Different agencies, each 'doing his own thing', provided sharply conflicting signals — sometimes intentionally, sometimes accidentally — about American conciliatory intentions or their absence. By all these explanations, the United States remained in Vietnam not because to do so in any way suited the national interest, but because particular policies suited the interests of particular agencies, frustrating coordinated understanding or execution.

Economic theories come in various shapes and sizes, all in one way or another attributing political and military acts to the needs of the American capitalist economy. In bare outline, some trace war to 'activities of the arms industries, 'merchants of death' in a military-industrial complex which promotes militarisation, internal hostility to justify military spending, and wars to require still more arms purchases. It may be hard to see how the defence industries alone (large in absolute sums of money spent, perhaps, but less than 10 per cent of the total economy) could determine vital decisions of war and peace. A more comprehensive version insists that the aggregate level of demand in the entire capitalist economy can be maintained only by excessive military spending, and that in turn requires a level of international tension and even active hostilies. Without military spending, it is alleged, the economy would collapse into depression.

More generally still, American capitalism is said to demand the defence of American markets or investments in Vietnam, Indochina and the rest of Southeast Asia. Of course such markets and investments are in fact minimal; less than 1 per cent of all United States foreign economic activity is directed to southeast Asia as a whole, and all United States foreign investment and sales together do not themselves exceed 15 per cent of total American productivity. The defence of economic interests in southeast Asia, then, is just too small a tail to wag such a very big dog. All sophisticated observers recognise this.

A less easily refutable version is an economic variant of dominoes, replete with demonstration effect. By this explanation, the purpose of American intervention was to prevent a nationalist or socialising regime from coming to power in Saigon not because South Vietnam was economically significant in itself, but as a clear warning to groups with similar aspirations in nations that were more significant. Nationalist takeovers in the less developed countries and attempts to remove those countries from the capitalist world economy would everywhere be resisted — better to make the case precisely where the immediate importance was minimal, so that American economic access could more easily and more peacefully be kept where it mattered. Again there remain problems with the relative size of the tail and the dog, especially in light of the rather modest proportion of all American investments and markets that are overseas, and the fact that less than one third of those are in less developed countries. Still, these theories can be made somewhat more plausible by emphasising the key nature of certain raw material supplies — for example, offshore oil deposits in the China Sea — or the peculiar political leverage of certain key pressure groups. Undoubtedly this kind of thinking went on in some people's minds, and the possibility of its importance should not be dismissed without examination.

Finally, there is a class of *ideological* theories that carry a certain persuasiveness. Certainly Cold War ideology, militant anti-communism, determined (sometimes hysterical) demands for resistance to communist expansion have played a part in American foreign policy. Even in the 1960s there remained in many quarters the vision of a fairly close, still quasi-monolithic world communism, headed by a Moscow-Peking axis that controlled dedicated instruments of war and subversion throughout the world. People with this vision typically were ideological conservatives on domestic American political issues.

They feared 'communist-inspired' economic 'levellers', dreaded communist subversion of democratic and capitalist institutions and favoured severe restrictions on civil liberties in order to control radicals and subversives. Anti-communist 'interventionist' policies thus would stem from a broad spectrum of interwoven beliefs, not limited to strategic or economic motivations. To some radicals anti-communist ideology is but a superstructure lending legitimacy and energy to policies directed to the protection of economic interests; without the interests the ideology could not be sustained. We may nevertheless cast the argument in a form not dependent on economic origins, of ideology as 'composed largely of symbols, visible in the public domain, with an independent capacity to influence behaviour'.[8]

An important variant of ideological theories, deserving separate attention, is that of *democratic* theories which stress the importance of ideology at the mass rather than the elite level of the political process. According to such theories, high level policy makers feared a backlash of militant anticommunism from the general populace in reaction to major foreign policy reverses. They remembered, for example, the domestic political cost of 'losing' China that were incurred by the Administration in the late 1940s, and the witch hunting of the Joseph McCarthy era which was so hard on liberals as well as radicals in the United States. In the words of Senator Sam Ervin recalling that time, 'You can't believe the terror that man [McCarthy] spread among politicians'.[9] Politicians feared to let loose a popular anti-communism which would punish them for foreign policy defeats, and were thus constrained by anti-communism even though they themselves were too sophisticated really to believe its premises. Believing that the people would not tolerate the 'loss' of Vietnam, senior elected and appointed officials in Washington therefore resolved that Vietnam would not be lost at least in their own terms in office. They would hang on, and escalate where necessary to avoid defeat, even though they knew the long term prospects for holding the country were poor. They could hope to postpone the day of reckoning to a time when they themselves would not be held responsible, and perhaps hope, against the evidence available to them, that events would break favourably so that the ultimate outcome would not be disastrous. According to some analysts, this kind of thinking can be found in every Administration from Truman to Nixon.[10]

Our example here is the Vietnam horror, but the different theoretical perspectives listed are of general interest and not limited to that set of events, nor to American foreign policy alone. They are general perspectives that could be applied to the policy orientation of almost any major power, with only some adaptations for the specific context. Similar reasoning could be applied to French policy in Indo-China or in Algeria, or for that matter to analysing the reasons for Soviet intervention in Czechoslovakia in 1968. Consider, for example, rationales about the power interests of the Soviet state, Brezhnev's problems of bureaucratic politics in the Kremlin, the distorting and possibly fear-inducing effects of communist ideology, and perhaps substitute, for economic interests, worries that the example of a parliamentary regime in Czechoslovakia would be its own kind of domino to endanger the communist political system throughout Eastern Europe. With appropriate adaptations these are virtually universal considerations applying to virtually all international actors.

Because they are indeed virtually universal, each of the kinds of theories carries substantial plausibility. As applied to Vietnam, each contains much that is persuasive, although a sophisticated observer would want to apply significant *caveats* or reservations to each. And evidence can be found to support each type of theory, at least in part. Doubtless each does in fact explain a part of the policy outcome. But that does not get us to a satisfactory scientific explanation, nor to an understanding that would permit us to predict the outcome of a similar set of pressures on another occasion for choice. Just because each has important elements of plausibility, we must ask with special vigour, what kinds of evidence would be required effectively to refute each theory? That is, what kind of evidence would establish that a particular kind of influence did not operate to affect the result? Or perhaps rather, only after conducting what kind of diligent search, where and how, *without* coming up with evidence to support the theory, could we then reliably regard the theory as refuted? If a theft has been committed, and the detective suspects the building was not entered from outside, it is not enough simply to establish that the doors remained locked. Until the windows too have been carefully checked, burglary remains a live hypothesis.

Still more important is the difficult question of evaluating the *relative* importance of each theory. Assuming as is likely that there is some evidence to support each, we cannot merely throw up our hands and express some vague notion of multiple causation. Some influences surely must matter more than others. Speaking quantitatively, how much of the variation in the total outcome, what percentage, can be accounted for by each explanation? An explanation accounting for half the variation is usually a good deal more interesting than one accounting for just two per cent. Thus what began as a policy problem and turned into a theoretical one now has become a problem of evidence — we cannot carry the discussion of theory much further without some attention to the question of what are the relevant pieces of evidence for testing various theories.

The Unintended Bias of Traditional Methods

Classical, 'traditional' methods of political and historical analysis concentrate on examining documents, personal and state papers, and memoires, supplemented by interviews with top policy makers where possible. They often ask what chief decision makers gave as the reasons for their policy and what motivations they attributed to other major actors. Overwhelmingly, the resulting statements stress strategic explanations, emphasising concern for power, security and national interest. It is, after all, a basic element of political myth that a top level leader, especially in democratic systems, is concerned for the national interest, must surmount narrow personal, group, or partisan interests which may motivate his constituents and must act, in terms of the American phrase, as 'President of all the people'. Top decision makers will invoke this kind of argument. When they do, they may well be describing their conscious motivations quite accurately; surely they do frequently think in such terms, for in their positions at the apex of so many conflicting pressures they have many reasons to take a broad overview.

But furthermore, they are encouraged by the myth to give such reasons and discouraged from emphasising other kinds of explanations. Presidents are unlikely, for instance, to stress the frustrations of bureaucratic politics. Of course they will mention some of their difficulties, and of the need for a President to present his wishes forcefully to his subordinates and to monitor their execution of his directives. Some appreciation of bureaucratic obstruction and self-interest is essential to any sympathetic evaluation of a President's lot in trying to carry out a coherent sustained policy for the general interest. Yet while Presidents want their difficulties to be appreciated, they rarely want to give the impression of having been overwhelmed by those difficulties. They will not want to give readers the impression of having been systematically unable to control their subordinates, or having been regularly duped by them. They hardly will want to risk looking like incompetent executives.

Nor certainly should anyone expect them to tell us much about economic interests and the kinds of parochial pressures to which they may have been subjected — especially where such pressures were successful. We recently have vividly seen how very reluctant policy makers are to disclose the activities of those who have lobbied them, or made political campaign contributions. Nor, finally, is any President or other top official likely to admit, however obliquely, that he put the priority of holding his office above the longer and broader term perspectives of the national interest. Louis XIV may have said 'après moi le déluge', but no democratic leader is about to admit he pursued that as a deliberate policy.

Mentioning these other possible motivations — bureaucratic conflict, economic interest, or considerations of democratic electoral politics — is not to imply that in any particular case, or even in most cases, these are the driving motivations behind the actions of major political figures. They may or may not be — but we are very unlikely ever to know merely by studying the kind of documentation and interview material that is publicly available, and especially the material publicly available on events within the past few decades. Substantial evidence supporting other interpretations is likely to emerge, if at all, only to future historians not operating within the constraints of contemporary security classification. Thus the absence of evidence supporting those interpretations cannot disprove the interpretations, since we should not expect to find much evidence there. The case necessarily remains open.

To probe further we can look at other kinds of documentary material, and interview and read the memoires of officials who operated below the very highest levels of the policy making process. The materials compiled by bureau chiefs, undersecretaries, ambassadors and speech-writers, and by journalists who have talked extensively with such people, are rich with explanations. But here again, the people involved are human, and must be expected to try to put a good face on their actions, to make themselves look reasonably good at the expense of their bureaucratic rivals. So here, in addition to perceptions of national interest, we would expect the mechanisms of deliberate or unconscious recall to emphasise the jungle of bureaucratic politics, and how their aims were thwarted by the narrow interests of others. Memoires by all the bureaucratic survivors (wounded and otherwise) from the Kennedy and Johnson years are full of this sort of material. Some men have returned to academia and they and their students, among others, have written fascinating and often deeply illuminating accounts of bureaucratic politics and the hazards to rational policy making. At the same time, economic and ideological influences do not figure prominently in these explanations. Sometimes they are mentioned, surely more often than by top level decision makers, but as exceptional cases and exceptional influences (always affecting *other* people's acts), not as pervasive factors. Again, we cannot make the mistake of assuming they *must* have operated, however sparse the evidence. But at the same time, the sparseness of evidence does not prove they did not operate; there is little reason to expect much such evidence to emerge, and much reason to expect ex-bureaucrats, especially frustrated ones or men who wish to disassociate themselves from unpopular policies, to tell us how red in tooth and claw are the struggles of bureaucratic politics.

Radical critics who wish to highlight the role of economic interests will, in their own way, also stress those kinds of evidence that will highlight the kinds of influence they think important. One variety of analysis examines aggregate data on foreign markets and investment patterns, showing the importance to key firms or industries of economic activities in countries that were the target of special political attention. It is practically always possible to find some such investment, sales, or import interest – but very difficult indeed to judge its importance in the political process, relative to a host of actual or potential countervailing interests.

Another type of analysis looks at particular cases of foreign policy decision making, and at the interests and connections of key participants. There are frequent enough cases where the coincidence of policy and of economic interests of the participants are more than suspiciously close, or even where direct action by economically-motivated actors can be identified beyond doubt. A notable example is the American military intervention of 1965 in the Dominican Republic, when many senior United States policy makers or advisors – Ellsworth Bunker, Adolf Berle, Abe Fortas – were officers or directors of big sugar companies. But especially in the American political system, the great majority of senior policy makers have close past or current corporate ties – as directors, officers, lawyers, shareholders, or at least relatives of same. It often becomes difficult not to find someone with an imputable corporate interest somehow in the outcome. Moreover, there are usually many other individuals without such apparent interests who can be found advocating similar policies. And as with Bunker in the Dominican case, it is not always those with the apparent economic interest who vigorously press the expected arguments, in this instance for intervention.

The matter is all very complicated, and it is rarely easy to trace an unambiguous causal sequence from interest to influence to decision. Indeed there are many cases where economically interested actors are known to have advocated self-serving policies, and failed utterly to carry them.[11] Despite the non-trivial number of American political and military interventions in the third world during recent decades, there are far more cases where the actual or imputed desires of economic interest groups would have pointed to interventions that in fact did not occur. Simply identifying examples and illustrations and interests, or even attempts to influence policy, will not suffice. Both a carefully developed theory of circumstances favouring or hindering the success of such efforts, and much additional information on perceptions, motivations and pressures, are required to bring predictive order into a

100

persuasive economic interpretation.

As a result, these traditional, classical tools of analysis cannot alone provide satisfactory answers to questions about the relative power of various kinds of influence on foreign policy making. Actually, the different pieces of evidence frequently slip past each other without ever meeting. One adviser may have an economic interest behind his advice, another may be moved in the same direction by ideological anti-communism, and yet another by 'hard-nosed' strategic considerations. If they all give the same recommendation and the President accepts, who had the 'real' power? These and other difficulties, all too familiar to close students of power and influence theory, bedevil the most careful and perceptive analyst. The analytical problems are extraordinarily difficult; bitter disputes over the relative importance of economic influences on foreign policy go back many years, at least to Hobson and the Marxists, and hardly seem closer to resolution now than in their early days. The fault does not stem from lack of insight or effort on the part of analysts. Politics is a very complex subject — 'harder than physics' — and this sort of problem especially difficult. But the problem is also an extremely important one; while we may never 'settle' these matters once and for all, they deserve better answers than have so far been devised. To get those answers we must ask somewhat different questions, and most importantly ask them in different ways, demanding different kinds of evidence.

The traditional methods are, by themselves, inadequate — not 'wrong', necessary in fact, but insufficient. They must be supplemented, especially because each of the basic traditional methods tends to be biased in terms of the kind of theories of world politics it tends to support. Some lead us to answers stressing strategic conceptions, others bureaucratic politics, others economic interests. These biases are rarely intended by the methods' practitioners; they seem the best and fairest that can be brought to bear on a particular decision or set of decision makers. But the biases, in terms of the kinds of evidence they find and cannot be expected to find, are there and, for the individual method by itself, virtually unavoidable. The evidence problem therefore has become a methodological one: how can we get the needed evidence, especially to test economic and ideological theories since they are probably the least satisfactorily investigated with the traditional methods?

Methods for Studying the Views of Corporate Executives

I know of no world-shaking solution to this problem, but I am currently pursuing a research project which tries to right the imbalance. In a variety of ways I am looking at the perceptions, attitudes, and preferences of major 'elite' groups, and especially those of high level executives of major corporate enterprises. I am asking whether their perceptions and preferences are significantly different from those of other elite groups, and how and on what kinds of foreign policy issues. I am comparing them systematically with other civilian and military elite groups, and where possibly examining changes over time. Among the large group of business executives, how do they differ among themselves? Do men employed by heavily defence-dependent firms differ markedly in their foreign policy orientation from that of executives in other industries? Similarly, is the orientation different for men from firms heavily dependent in underdeveloped countries? Do they express economic motivations, and are these motivations then related to the choice of particular policies, as for intervention or the support of certain kinds of regimes in less developed countries? Or is policy choice related less to economic interest or motivation than to 'ideological' liberal-conservative differences on domestic policy, or to conceptions about strategy and international power relationships?[12]

I do not for a moment imagine that beliefs, preferences and attitudes about politics are to be equated with political acts, influence attempts, or the successful exercise of political power. All these latter give rise to other questions requiring very different inquiries and evidence. This is not a search to find who has power, who makes decisions, certainly not who constitutes a 'power elite' over what foreign policy issues. Questions about power and its exercise surely are not trivial; they remain some of the most central questions of political science. But they are extraordinarily difficult questions. Probably no aspect of political science has been analysed so thoroughly as has the problem of power, with such

102

indeterminate empirical results. Efforts to establish convincingly the existence and scope of a power elite, for example, have generally failed to be convincing by the standard criteria of empirical social science. Partly this is the result of conceptual, theoretical difficulties in the approach, but at least as much it is due to the extremely complex and abstruse nature of the world at issue. Especially when power is defined as the ability to get someone to do something he would not otherwise do, the barriers to establishing such hypothetical circumstances are virtually insuperable. These same barriers bedevil the pluralist critics of power elite theories. However cogent their critiques or ingenious their counterpropositions, it remains almost impossible ever to prove there is *not* a power elite, or even at the more modest level that economically-motivated individuals do not exert great power over decision making. These are very interesting, but extremely difficult matters for investigation. We might for a while avoid them, not out of disrespect for their importance, but out of respect for their difficulty.

Instead, I have moved to a logically *prior* step of enquiry. By asking about the beliefs, preference and attitudes of corporate executives, I am trying to discover whether those attitudes are consistent with what various theorists about economic or other motivations would have us expect. In what ways do businessmen think differently about foreign policy than do other leaders, and what kinds of differences, associated with what sort of ideological or economic characteristics, exist within the business community? By addressing a few central matters about motivations, an enquiry could in principle serve almost as a 'critical experiment' to determine the direction of future investigation into questions about economic influence. If the attitudes are such as would be predicted by economic influence theories, then there will be good reason to redouble efforts to trace the exercise of power and influence. If on the contrary the attitudes do not bear much resemblance to those predicted, then it may be time to move on to other kinds of more promising enquiries.

In the project I have explored these questions first through a sample survey conducted of top level executives, with the results compared with those from similar surveys of other elite individuals. I asked a wide range of questions, hoping to tap their attitudes in suitably subtle and mixed ways. The individuals concerned are highly intelligent; the task of inquiring into their beliefs with reasonably accurate results is far from easy. There are serious limits on the ability of survey research to tap complicated matters with sophisticated respondents, and I was obliged to supplement the large scale survey results with substantial numbers of face to face intensive interviews, testing the validity of the survey responses and developing some of the subtle undertones. But the survey approach has great advantages as well as hazards attached to it; with a sufficiently large and well-designed sample it becomes possible to generalise statistically about the relative effect of various influences with a confidence that can never be achieved from a score or two of interviews, however intensive and probing. The two methods again are not mutually exclusive, but mutually supportive when used in tandem.

Another methodological approach of this project has been to look intensively at what businessmen say to each other, or more precisely at what journalists say to businessmen through the medium of their specialised business and financial press. What policy recommendations do writers make, based on what kind — economic, ideological, strategic — of justifications? How have these changed over recent decades, in response to different kinds of international events, and how do they compare with the kind of political recommendations and justifications to be found, for example, in journals edited for and by military men?

Finally, I looked in some detail at share prices on the New York stock exchange, how they have moved up and down in apparent response to various international events, and particularly to war-related events during the Korean and Indochina conflicts. Stock prices can serve as one indicator of expectations, in the business and financial community, of how major segments of the economy may fare as a result of international developments. Has the market been 'bullish' or 'bearish' in response to escalatory events during the wars, or in response to conciliatory acts by either side? Has the pattern varied over time, either between the two wars or during the course of either? Perhaps more importantly, have particular kinds of stocks, such as those of defence-oriented firms, or of firms with heavy stakes in the less developed countries, behaved differently from those of most other firms? Used cautiously and with discrimination, stock prices become one more

104

partial indicator of attitudes and beliefs in the corporate world.

Together all these pieces of evidence should give us some information of a sort previously unavailable. None of these pieces is by itself unassailable; serious questions can and should be raised about the validity of each. Scepticism is appropriate about the interpretations put on changes in stock prices, or about how much candour we really can expect in the business and financial press, or about the profundity of survey research. There are many pitfalls, and an enormous technical literature associated with each. No one scholar can master all, though by being willing to seek expert advice, and working with others, quite a few pitfalls can be avoided. As noted, similar questions, no less searching, can be raised about the validity of interviewing or documentary analysis of the kind of material usually available to journalists or historians. The aim is not to replace traditional analysis with the newer sorts of material, but merely to supplement, to complement, the conclusions obtainable through the more traditional methods. By drawing on multiple streams of evidence, each with its own limitations but also with its own strengths in terms of the kinds of evidence it is likely to uncover, we can extend our understanding of these very complex yet important political phenomena. A scholar equipped only with traditional methods, or only with quantitative methods, is like a student of the ancient world who knows Greek but not Latin, or Latin but not Greek. One will suffice to answer many questions, but many others require both.

This attempt to bring new kinds of evidence to bear in some ways resembles the different things one 'sees' by 'looking' in various ways at the human body. By looking with your eyes in ordinary light, you see the colour and texture of the surface; skin, hair, clothing. But by looking with heat-sensitive infra-red instruments, you see varied patterns of warmth, spots and periods of intense activity, others at rest. Or by looking at an X-ray picture, you see the basic underlying structure of support, strength, and vulnerability. None of these is 'the' picture of the human body, but each tells us very different things about how it functions, what its capabilities are, and what to expect of it. Methodological eclecticism is valuable not for its own sake, but to broaden understanding in directions that the traditional methods cannot so easily reach.

And the questions *are* important, from a policy-oriented viewpoint where we began, as well as from one concerned with theory. If economic interests have truly been powerful influences impelling American intervention in Vietnam and elsewhere in the underdeveloped world, then presumably they could produce the same effect again, on an occasion where the prospective cost-benefit ratio looked more favourable. If economic pressures have been powerful, then the possibility of 'imperial' rivalry with other economically-motivated major powers exists for the future. If strategic considerations were paramount, then diminished world bipolarity and the rise of new power centres will somehow, in ways not always easy to discern, affect future willingness to intervene on behalf of strategic power. If ideology, or the fear of an ideologically-motivated mass public, was paramount, then maybe there are special grounds for optimism that future interventions can be more readily avoided. There is substantial evidence of a major shift in ideology, a shift that has left vast numbers of people, especially of a younger generation, devoid of many of the fears and ideologically-motivated ambitions of the Cold War years. Whatever the facts, one's prescriptions for how to avoid a repetition of past tragedies will depend centrally on the diagnosis of why past ones occurred. We cannot comprehend future world politics until we understand how people view their past and present.

References

1. See Chapter 2, Bruce M. Russett, 'A Macroscopic View of International Politics', in my *Power and Community in World Politics* (San Francisco': W.H. Freeman, 1974), for a more general argument about the long term stabilities in the structure of world politics.
2. For a well-documented review of the rationales, see F.M. Kahl, *What Washington Said: Administration Rhetoric and the Vietnam War* (New York: Harper and Row, 1973).
3. *Gallup Opinion Index,* Report No. 39, September 1968, p. 3.
4. While I arrived at this basic four-fold scheme independently, it is remarkably similar to that of James Kurth, as laid out in his 'Aerospace Production Lines

and American Defence Spending', in Steven Rosen, ed., *Testing the Theory of the Military-Industrial Complex* (Lexington, Mass: D.C. Heath, 1973), and 'The Multinational Corporation, U.S. Foreign Policy, and the Underdeveloped World', in Steven Rosen, ed. *Testing the Economic Theory of Imperialism* (Lexington, Mass: D.C. Heath, 1974). We will draw rather heavily in the following discussion on some of Kurth's incisive comments.

5. For some representative quotations by American leaders, using the Munich analogy after World War II, see Bruce M. Russett, *No Clear and Present Danger: A Sceptical View of the United States Entry into World War II* (New York: Harper and Row, 1972), pp. 83-5.

6. Theories of national interest and concern for power are extremely common. The most influential among academics, and probably on policy makers as well, is doubtless Hans J. Morgenthau, *Politics Among Nations* (New York: Knopf, first edition 1948). Certainly one sees it in Lyndon B. Johnson, *The Vantage Point: Perspectives on the Presidency* (New York: Holt, 1971).

7. The argument on size is well expressed by Anthony J. Downs, *Inside Bureaucracy* (Boston: Little Brown, 1967). The recent surge of academic interest in the effects of bureaucratic politics begins with Richard Neustadt, *Alliance Politics* (New York: Columbia University Press, 1970) and was given further impetus by Graham Allison, *Essence of Decision: Explaining the Cuban Missile Crisis* (Boston: Little Brown, 1971). On the Kennedy-Johnson administrations in general, and on Vietnam in particular, see the books by various participants: Schlesinger, Sorensen, Hilsman, Cooper, Hooper, McNamara, *et al.* A useful interpretation is David Halberstam, *The Best and the Brightest* (London: Barrie and Jenkins, 1972).

8. Douglas Rosenberg, 'Arms and the American Way', in Bruce M. Russett and Alfred Stepan, eds., *Military Force and American Society* (New York: Harper and Row, 1972) p. 160.

9. Seminar at Yale University, 13 February 1974.

10. This seems basically to be the interpretation of Daniel Ellsberg, 'The Quagmire Myth and the Stalemate Machine', *Public Policy*, 19, 2 (Spring 1971), pp. 217-74. See also Leslie Gelb, 'Vietnam: The System Worked', *Foreign Policy*, no. 3 (Summer 1971), and Halberstam *op. cit.* To an important degree this popular anticommunism was built up by policy makers themselves, as in Senator Vandenberg's advice to Truman that he must 'go and scare hell out of the country'. Once this force was unleashed, policy makers felt more constrained by it than they wished.

11. For various examples of both successful and unsuccessful efforts Anthony Sampson, *Sovereign State. The Secret History of ITT* (London, 1973). is illuminating. See also the brief but useful discussion in Kurth, 'The Multinational Corporations', *op. cit.*

12. See Bruce M. Russett and Betty C. Hanson, *Interest and Ideology: The Foreign Policy Beliefs of American Businessmen* (forthcoming, 1975). The answers are as complex as the questions, and defy easy summarisation. In the briefest statement, nevertheless, my survey evidence indicates that while economic influences do operate they are generally overshadowed by ideological ones. Those economic influences for which we have evidence

typically 'explain' two per cent or less of businessmen's foreign policy perspectives; ideological characteristics explain about ten per cent, sometimes much more. Similarly, in the stock market analysis stock prices' response to events in the Korean War and the early years of Vietnam were essentially random; in the later years they were opposite to what economic theories would predict. The content analysis was still not complete at this time of writing, so for the full answer both author and reader will have to wait for the book.

6 THE PROBLEM OF EVALUATING WAR

Inis L. Claude

Throughout recorded history, war has been one of the most noteworthy of human activities. It has attracted, and continues to attract, vast quantities of attention. Historians, from Thucydides to Michael Howard, and poets, from Homer to Betjeman, have written about it. In their various ways, such diverse groups as toymakers, heads of government, monument builders, scientists, songwriters, industrialists, clergymen, professors of international relations and clothing designers (those who plan the sartorial fads that erupt spontaneously from time to time) join generals and admirals in displaying interest in war. Preoccupation with this phenomenon is to be observed in Hollywood, the Pentagon, Tin Pan Alley, Turtle Bay and the Harvard Yard; in Whitehall, St Paul's Cathedral, Fleet Street and the studios of the BBC.

War grips our attention because it is laden with dramatic quality; one need only consult the titles given by Bruce Catton to his volumes about the American Civil War, or by Churchill to his volumes about World War II, to discover the conception of war as tragedy on a massive scale. Whenever two or more old soldiers are gathered together, it is revealed that war is also a comedy of errors. To an enormous extent, the peoples of the world derive from war their stocks of heroes and villains, their tales of glory and shame, their conceptions of darkest days and finest hours and their sets of national landmarks and historic turning points. Since World War II, there can hardly have been a moment when somebody, somewhere, was not saying or writing the phrase 'since World War II'. War strikes us as momentous, decisive, and explosive. It brings human passions to a point of extraordinary intensity and magnifies almost every vice and virtue known to man. Love and hate, cruelty and tenderness, selfishness and sacrifice, devotion and betrayal, discipline and chaos, ruthlessness and restraint . . . all of these are intimately associated with war.

Over the centuries, war has aroused mixed reactions. Thucydides gave this speech to Hermocrates of Syracuse, during the Peloponnesian War: 'That war is an evil is a proposition so familiar to everyone that it would be tedious to develop it'.[1] To this day, men have continued to denounce and deplore war. Throughout the same period, war has been justified and glorified. Pericles' Funeral Oration and Lincoln's Gettysburg Address have honoured the dead, and the eloquent speeches of Wilson and Churchill have inspired the living to seek nobility in martial exploits. War has been condemned as a manifestation of barbarism and praised as an incubator of civic virtues. War is hell — but a special heaven is reserved for its heroes. It has been regarded as destructive of all that men should value, and as productive and protective of civilisation's finest fruits. It has been held to represent man at his worst and at his best, to bring out the beast and to call forth the saint. War's capacity to dominate human attention is exceeded only by its capacity to generate ambivalence in the human breast.

On the face of it, the reaction of those who now think seriously about war is marked by an unprecedented emancipation from ambivalence. War, for excellent reasons, has become very unpopular in our time. Hard lessons and terrible dangers have made pacifists, of some sort, of us all. We tend to regard war as unadulterated horror, unmitigated folly and unmixed evil. It is unthinkable, intolerable and insupportable. We find it difficult to believe that sane and humane public figures, only a short while ago, could have praised war as a salutary social exercise, or to acknowledge that the *real* people of democratic societies, as distinguished from cabals of scheming warlords, have sometimes pressed for military adventures. The more deeply one is convinced that no right-thinking person can avoid the absolute condemnation of war, the stronger is the temptation to apply that conviction retroactively. Anti-war doctrine has recently become a powerful orthodoxy, particularly in Western countries.

While the development of this orthodoxy is not primarily attributable to academic specialists in international relations, its impact has been felt within our scholarly fraternity. The formal study of international

110

relations began in the twentieth century less as a scientific enterprise than as a reformist movement, and the prevention of war has persistently ranked high among the objectives of scholars in this field. It is noteworthy that much more attention has been devoted to analysis of the causes than to study of the effects of war. This perhaps reflects the assumption that the effects are all too evident, and too uniformly horrible, to require examination; knowing that war is bad, we need only to learn how to prevent it, and that of course requires that we understand its causes. The academic discipline of international relations, predisposed to treat war as a problem to be solved, is highly susceptible to pressures to treat war as the *only* problem deserving its concentrated attention and, beyond that, to approach war in the spirit of one who crusades against evil. The influence of these pressures can be seen in the rather widespread substitution of the title 'peace research' for the more conventional 'study of international relations'. This change of title is not, I think, a mere semantic variation; it seems to me to be intended to connote the narrowing of the field and the subordination of analysis to advocacy, the transformation of the study of international relations into a campaign to eliminate the evil of war. Peace research is thus conceived as an auxiliary of the pacifist movement, and its practitioners are valued as intellectual advisers to, if not active participants in, that movement.

This development has an unfortunate tendency to promote the ideological polarisation of the academic group concerned with international affairs. Scholars who decline membership in the peace research fraternity are likely to be condemned as warmongers or, at best, to be regarded as morally indifferent fellows who are content to indulge in academic fiddling while Rome burns. They, being all too human, are inclined to respond with nasty cracks about 'peaceniks'.

This controversy raises fundamental questions about the relationship between scholarship and ideology. *Can* scholars divorce their intellectual activity from their commitments to values and causes? *Should* they do so? The answers to these two questions are not wholly separable. The peace researcher tends to answer both questions in the negative, and his second negative is in part a product of his first. Since we cannot avoid bending our scholarship to our normative concerns, it is better neither to

111

pretend nor to try to do so. If one is devoted to a worthy cause, why not turn one's intellectual talents to its service, frankly and proudly? From this point of view, the student who purports to engage in disinterested scholarship is guilty either of self-deception or of the effort to conceal his true ideological colours, and he who attempts to confine himself to objective analysis makes his work irrelevant to the real world and reveals himself as a political eunuch.

The nonadherent to the peace research school has a rather more complicated position. He doubts that one can, but insists that one should try to keep his commitments out of his scholarship. What this comes to is the conviction that value free scholarship is an unattainable but an approachable ideal, and that the scholar's obligation is to keep as close to that ideal as constant effort can take him. Commitment taints scholarship; it is to be regretted and combatted. Whereas the peace researcher's belief in the impossibility of objectivity strengthens his tendency to regard it as undesirable, his opposite number moves from conviction that objectivity is desirable to belief that, within limits, it is possible. To the accusation that he evades moral responsibility by striving for uncommitted scholarship, he offers several responses. First, he asserts his commitment to the socially valuable cause of dispassionate scholarship. During the struggle within the United States over Vietnam, for instance, he felt that it was more important for the long term health of American society for universities to preserve and defend their status as citadels of objective scholarship than for them to serve as organising centres for political action. Secondly, he asserts the necessity of attempting the admittedly difficult task of separating his scholarly from his personal role, taking every possible precaution to prevent his performance as scholar from being distorted by his commitments as human being, or as citizen. Ultimately, he believes that scholars who are resolutely committed to a wide ranging examination of the complexities of international relations and a quest for balanced understanding of that field will contribute more to the laying of firm foundations upon which dedicated human beings can build a structure of peace than will scholars who put their intellectual activity deliberately and directly to the service of a campaign against war.

I associate myself with the latter of these two positions. I undertake to study international relations. The study of war — its causes, its characteristics and its effects — is an important part, but not the whole, of that undertaking. As a human being, I want to prevent war. As a student, I want to understand it — and I believe that understanding is more important than aversion as preparation for the effort to reduce the impact of war upon mankind. I think that the general study of international relations will contribute more to our understanding of war than the special study of war can contribute to our understanding of international relations. I am reluctant to have the study of war dominate the study of international relations to the exclusion of all else — and I am concerned about the danger that the antiwar obsession may distort our study of international relations.

The first order of business is to gain an understanding of the aversion to war that is so prominent a feature of presentday mentality. We need to engage in a calm and careful examination of our attitudes toward war. How *should* we evaluate it? How *do* we, in fact, feel about war? I propose to argue that current antiwar doctrine is excessive in two ways: it presents an evaluation of war that is more negative than the facts warrant, and it overstates the actual antipathy of its adherents to war. It is, in short, both false and misleading. The 'bandwagon' mentality has been at work. Criticism of war has been superseded by passionate denunciation, the pressure for conformity has demanded uncritical acceptance and repetition of antiwar assertions, and the momentum of exaggeration has become irresistible. Who dares to deny any allegation about the wickedness or folly or futility of war? Who permits himself even to think that war may not be an absolute evil? This is where the need for dispassionate scholarship intrudes. We must seek the truth about war and confront our own judgements about it, stripped of their rhetorical exaggerations, before we can settle down to the task of devising sensible approaches to the problems that it poses. The function of real scholarship is always to challenge orthodoxy, even the orthodoxy of dissenters, and to press the orthodox to be honest with himself about the nature of his convictions. The true believer must be forced to ask whether what he believes is true and whether he truly believes it. The proposition that the scholar's proper role is less to answer questions than to question answers is nowhere more valid than in the case of today's antiwar orthodoxy.

If, in our condemnation of war, we are guilty of going beyond both what is true and what we believe to be true, this excess must be traced primarily to the overloading of that poor little word *war*. It is convenient, for certain purposes, to have a single and singular noun to designate all the violent struggles that occur among large and organised human groups, but *war* serves us badly when it tempts us to lump together all the varieties of military conflict and to generalise about them, as if they were simply multiple examples of the same phenomenon.

The beginning of wisdom about war, as about so many other concepts in our field, is the recognition that it is plural, not singular — the discarding of the illusion of the homogeneity of its content. The analytically crucial 's' must be added; war consists of *wars*. I suggest two approaches to the pluralisation of the concept of war.

The first approach concentrates on categorising wars — and on keeping in mind, and taking into account, the differentiation among them that is implied by the act of sorting them out according to type. I claim no originality in suggesting that one can usefully distinguish between global and local wars, thermonuclear and conventional wars, all out and limited wars, international and internal or civil wars, declared and ambiguous wars, planned and inadvertent wars, wars of attrition and wars quickly concluded, and so forth. These are imperfect categories, in some instances serving to mark the end points of a continuum rather than to establish a sharp dichotomy. Moreover, these examples do not exhaust the list of possible classifications. They may suffice, however, to remind us of the importance of caution in generalising about war.

In truth, our problem is not that we are unaware of the fact that wars differ significantly from each other, but that we fail to keep that fact consistently in mind. We would have nothing but disdain for a defence minister or staff officer who betrayed the belief that all wars require the same equipment and strategy, but we ourselves tend to ignore the differences among wars when we pass judgement on *war*. Is it any more sensible to say that war settles or achieves nothing, or that it puts the entire fabric of civilisation at risk, or that it is incompatible with fundamental moral principles, than to say that it requires the total mobilisation of the national economy, or the imposition of universal military service, or the nuclear destruction of the enemy's cities, or the training of a large contingent of ski troops, or the provision of a fleet of amphibious landing craft? *Which* war is one talking about? To *what kind* of war does one refer? For the critic and evaluator of war, quite as much as for the government official in charge of military plans and preparations, it is necessary to consider the implications of the heterogeneity of the phenomena that we cover with the terminological blanket of war. We must control our tendency to move from the conviction that an all out thermonuclear conflict is unthinkable to the proposition that *war* is unthinkable, from the belief that the Vietnam war settled nothing to the view that *war* settles nothing, and from the premise that World War I was foolish and unnecessary to the conclusion that war is an irrational act. Passionate ideologues and ambitious political theory builders incite each other to more and more prodigious feats of generalisation about war. It is time for all of us to join in a campaign of de-generalisation. There is not very much to be said about *a* war that applies with equal validity to *all* wars. The concept of war serves us best as a general heading that invites immediate departure into typological analysis. We will find it safer, most of the time, to keep our attention fixed upon the subheads.

My second suggestion for coping with the errors fostered by the use of war as a singular noun involves the cracking of the unity of each individual conflict. For some purposes, it undoubtedly makes sense to consider a war as a whole. There are some things that can properly and usefully be said about the historical significance, or the systemic effects, or the circumstances leading to the outbreak, of the Russo-Japanese War, the Spanish Civil War, or World War II. But the notion of the unity of a war has only limited validity. For a great many purposes — and especially for assessing the justification for fighting and the value of its results — it is essential not only to distinguish a particular war from others but also to divide it into its component parts. Every war is, in fact, at least two wars; the A-B war comprises the war of A against B and the war of B against A. The implications of the dualism, or the pluralism, of every (apparently) single war deserve our most careful attention.

Evaluative comment about the war of A against B is more likely to imply the reverse than the same judgement of the war of B against A. For instance, if we denounce A's war as an illegal campaign of aggression, or an immoral effort to perpetuate colonialism, we are likely to consider B's war a proper exercise of the legal right of self-defence, or a worthy assertion of the right of national self-determination. If A attempts to subvert the independence of B but suffers enormous losses and ultimate defeat, we may conclude that A's war was foolish and counterproductive, while judging that B's war was well worth what it cost. Note that none of these suppositions encourages the view that we can offer a valid judgement of the legality, the morality, the rationality, or the profitability of the hypothetical A-B war; we can evaluate the two halves separately, but not in combination.

The proposition that every war is a composite, each segment of which should be evaluated separately, and the expectation that a favourable evaluation of one segment will require an unfavourable evaluation of the other, are strongly entrenched in formal thought about international relations. Traditional just war theory, in so far as it focuses on just cause for war, reflects both this proposition and this expectation. It does not sort wars into just and unjust categories, but devides a bilateral war into just and unjust halves — and treats the lack of justification for one half as the basis of justification for the other. In so far as just war theory concerns itself with the conduct of war, it may, of course, condemn either or both sides for improper behaviour — but even in this case it performs a separate examination of each of the wars that together constitute the 'whole' war. Just war theory has nothing to say about the Franco-Prussian War; it may have distinct, and contrasting things to say about France's war against Prussia and about Prussia's war against France.

One sees this same approach in Hans Kelsen's legal theory. For Kelsen, the use of force is either a delict or a sanction. sanction. presupposes delict, and is defined as a legal response to illegal violence. Thus, Kelsen could not conceive of a legal or an illegal war, in the composite sense; he had to look for the law-breaking and the law-upholding parts of the whole encounter.

The theory of collective security, imperfectly embodied in the Covenant of the League of Nations and the Charter of the United Nations, follows this line. In a fully fledged collective security system, every war would be divided into legally prohibited, legally permitted and legally required segments. One party, A, would be condemned for committing aggression against B; B would be permitted to defend itself against A; C, D and the rest would be obliged to join the fight against A. Moreover, the rationality as well as the legality of war is treated in discriminating fashion by collective security theory. Rejecting the simple notion that 'war does not pay', the theory holds that war *does* pay, unless it is met by counterwar that imposes costs sufficient to make it unprofitable. The conviction that aggressive war will pay must be shattered by the realisation that the community is determined to prevent it from paying. States must be motivated by confidence that it does pay to conduct war, under community auspices, to demonstrate that war, against the order of the community, does not pay. This is the essence of the scheme of collective security.

Both the League and the United Nations have proved disappointing to collective security enthusiasts, but they have substantially adopted the attitude toward war described above. It is nonsense to say that the Covenant and the Charter make war illegal. They both envisage the development of arrangements under which the various parties in a given war will be collectively judged to be fighting in violation of law, in exercise of the legally acknowledged right of self-defence, or in fulfilment of the legal obligation to support international order. Despite the abandonment of any real commitment to operating a collective security system within the framework of the United Nations, members frequently press the organisation to discriminate between opposing sides in armed conflicts and continue to argue about the allocation of its official blessings and curses. When the United Nations is used as an agency for passing legal or moral judgement upon a war, its pronouncements relate to the merits of particular segments of that war.

I do not mean to advocate the adoption of such a judgemental approach to all wars. Most conflicts are not simple confrontations of

117

guilty attackers and innocent victims. Political organs of international organisations are ill-suited to render even-handed judgements in cases of military conflict, and multilateral debate on the relative merits of combatants may be both a waste of time and a misapplication of institutional resources. It is surely more important to stop a war than to reach agreement about who started it. If we are to deal intelligently and constructively with the problem of war in our time, I believe that we must incline toward regarding war less as a function of the policy of states and more as a function of their predicament. We should concentrate less on the problem of aggression and more on the problem of rivalry, and our emphasis should shift from the *who* to the *what* as we search for the causes of war. Hence, I am not convinced that the collapse of prospects for creating a collective security system is altogether a bad thing, or that the use of United Nations organs to distribute praise and blame among parties in conflict is altogether a good thing. In short, there is much to be said for treating whole wars as tragedies to be prevented, rather than for regarding parts of wars as crimes to be punished. Nevertheless, a great deal of 'taking sides' is inescapable. Governments frequently range themselves on one side or the other when armed conflicts occur and, as critics or supporters of the policy of our own and other governments, we find ourselves adopting partisan positions with respect to those conflicts. It is important that we be aware of, and frank about, what we are doing. We have drifted into the lazy habit of purporting to oppose war, when we actually oppose only one segment of a war. This means that we denounce war more sweepingly and vehemently than we should, or than we really intend to do.

There are, unfortunately, ample precedents for this behaviour. In November 1915, President Wilson set forth a plan for strengthening the armed forces of the United States, with the comment: 'We have it in mind to be prepared, not for war, but only for defence.'[2] Surely, he meant that the United States intended to use its armed forces, if necessary, for *defensive* war. By declining to include fighting for defence of what he regarded as legitimate American interests under the rubric of war, Wilson encouraged the belief, which he did not share, that war *per se* is unjustifiable. He was actually speaking in support of

118

engagement in the defensive half of an aggressor-defender conflict, but he allowed himself to seem an opponent of the whole of such a war.

The Kellogg-Briand Pact provides another example of this kind of loose verbiage. It purported to prohibit the use of war as an instrument of national policy, and it has served as a favourite citation for those who think that they are thoroughgoing opponents of war. In fact, this document approved the use of war as an instrument of defensive policy; it did not so much prohibit war as attempt to indicate the kinds of policy that should and should not be pursued by military means. As Michael Howard has pointed out, 'The state which defends itself against invasion is using war as an instrument of policy no less than the invader.'[3]

Perhaps the most striking and significant illustration of our contemporary tendency to confuse condemnation of part of a war with opposition to the entire war and — by extension — to war itself, is afforded by the activity of those, in the United States and elsewhere, who condemned American involvement in Vietnam. They regarded themselves as being 'against the war in Vietnam', and the characterisation of their campaign as 'the antiwar movement' has been widely accepted.

This characterisation requires critical appraisal. Their opposition was concentrated upon the American and South Vietnamese component of the Vietnam war, with emphasis upon the American involvement; *that* was immoral, illegal, unreasonable, unnecessary and unconscionable. They did not conspicuously oppose the other half of that war. Indeed, they objected to opposing the other half; the central complaint against the United States was precisely that it did intervene to affect the outcome of the effort to eliminate South Vietnam as a separate entity. In so far as they advocated allowing the other half of the war to succeed, they did not display the belief that war does not pay but undertook to help make it a paying proposition. If any group in the United States could be said to have opposed the *whole* Vietnam war, it was the 'hawks', not the 'doves', for the former favoured the simultaneous termination of the two halves and the latter were interested only in the ending of American participation.

It is not my purpose to assess the merits of the case for and against the role of the United States in the Vietnamese conflict. I cite it only to make the point that attitudes toward war today are often not what

119

they seem. There are some absolute pacifists to be found, but they are not numerous and it is not my impression that they are dominant in the so-called antiwar movement. For most members of that group, as for most human beings at all times and places, approval of resort to violence is to be bestowed selectively, in accordance with one's sympathies and loyalties and one's conception of what constitutes a just cause. I am not convinced that those who self-consciously associate themselves with today's antiwar orthodoxy surpass all others in their devotion to the general ideal of promoting world peace, or in their effectiveness as contributors to the realisation of that ideal. Most of us deplore the necessity of fighting in a good cause, but we confine our condemnation to those who create, exempting those who respond to, that necessity. We should like to eliminate war, but we think that it is right and proper for people to fight in defence, or even in promotion, of interests and values that strike us as legitimate. Our disagreements relate not to that principle, but to the details of its application to real situations: What interests and values are worthy of violent defence or promotion? What circumstances provide moral and rational justification for resort to force on behalf of those interests and values? Whose military activity, in a given situation, deserves approbation or disapprobation? Above all, how can we prevent the development of situations that, in our view, necessitate and justify violence? This, I think, is a far more accurate picture of our situation than is presented by those who ask us to envisage an heroic band of antiwar activists struggling against an establishment enamoured of, or indifferent to, war.

The pluralisation of the concept of war that I have advocated — that is, the recognition of the implications of the differences among wars and the divisions within them — is an important step toward clarification and refinement of our reaction to the general phenomenon of war. It does not, however, solve all the problems involved in our undertaking. The historical persistence of ambivalent attitudes should alert us to the intrinsic difficulty of evaluating war. We shall go astray if we take the ambivalence of past generations to mean merely that our ancestors were, in all too many cases, insufficiently endowed with good sense and good will to see war as the evil that it was and is. Moral sensitivity and clear rationality are not innovations of the late twentieth century, and it is not a safe assumption that our time has produced even a notable upsurge in the incidence of these admirable qualities. Generational self-righteousness deserves as little respect now as in any previous time. We shall be well advised to regard the mixed reactions of the past to war — which, as I have argued, we share to a greater degree than we generally realise or admit — as evidence not of the moral or intellectual deficiency of the reactors but of the complexity of the phenomenon to which they have reacted. War is, if not a many splendoured thing, at least a multifaceted thing.

I take it for granted that the only sensible way to evaluate war — a particular war, or wars in general — is to develop a cost-benefit analysis. A balance sheet must be drawn up, and one must formulate a judgement as to whether costs exceed benefits or benefits outweigh costs. With regrettable frequency we make or encounter evaluations that are based upon awareness or consideration of only one side of the balance sheet: positive evaluations that reflect no calculation of the costs, and negative evaluations that reflect no appreciation of the benefits. This, clearly, will not do. Cost-benefit analysis presents many problems, not the least of which is the difficulty of determining the value to be assigned to the disparate elements that appear on the two sides of the ledger. How does one compare the significance of death and destruction with that of the achievement of national unity or the maintenance of national independence, for instance? There are no easy or objective answers to such questions, and we would be foolish to expect general agreement. But each of us must answer them as best he can. No one has a right to be taken seriously when he pronounces upon the justifiability of a war or of war in general unless he has asked and attempted to answer the questions: what are the costs and the benefits, and which side outweighs the other?

Quite aside from the problem of assessing the relative weight of costs and benefits, once one has lined them up for consideration, there are enormous difficulties in getting, and knowing that one has got a full and accurate listing of the elements that should be entered into the equation. At least in the short run, the danger of omission is greater for benefits than for costs.

While there may be long term costs that cannot be anticipated, the immediate costs of war are so obvious – so striking, so painful and disturbing, so tangible in many though not in all instances – that they are unlikely to be overlooked. One can achieve at least a rough count of dead and wounded and put some sort of monetary figure on military expenditures and damage to property. There are, of course, other costs that cannot be measured, but many of them are likely to make a deep imprint upon our consciousness, even while a war is in progress. For instance, no thoughtful American can fail to be aware of the extraordinary costs of an unquantifiable, nonmaterial sort that we suffered during and in connection with the Vietnam war. I believe that the danger of seriously underestimating the costs of war today is relatively slight.

By contrast, the benefit of war are more elusive. They tend to be less tangible, less measurable, and less demonstrable. What one achieves in war is often speculative; it may consist in preventing what one suspects would have happened if the war had not been fought or if one had been defeated, or in paving the way for what one hopes will happen in the distant future. Such remote, uncertain and unprovable benefits as these obviously cannot compete on equal terms with direct and undeniable costs in the struggle for popular recognition.

'I *know* that my son was killed, my city was smashed, and my taxes were doubled to pay for this war; you tell me that you *believe* we averted a serious threat to our security and *hope* that the world will be more stable in the future? I *know* that we have killed and maimed thousands of people, and destroyed vast numbers of homes, shops and factories; you tell me that you *believe* that we have enhanced the prospects for political freedom in that country?'

Such scepticism may be as unwarranted as it is inevitable; *knowing* what good war has done and what evil it has prevented is almost impossible. The benefits of war seldom bear upon a population in so intimate, clear and immediate a way as do the costs. Pericles indicated this when he spoke to the Athenians during a difficult phase of the Peloponnesian War: 'The suffering that it entails is being felt by everyone among you, while its advantage is still remote and obscure . . .'[4] The costs of fighting are seen and felt. The costs of *not* fighting are a matter of conjecture and controversy. It is a relatively simple matter for anyone bent upon proving that war does not pay to dismiss as nonsense virtually all claims and hopes of valuable results.

The normal tendency for the contemporary record of a war to give fuller play to costs than to benefits is enhanced by the new factor of television. I have in mind the performance of TV in Vietnam, which brought the visible reality of war home, quite literally, to the American public. The nation had a closeup view of death and destruction that it had not seen for a hundred years. I believe that the combination of two factors — the absence of large scale fighting from our territory since the Civil War, and the presence of the television set in the contemporary living room — goes far toward explaining the reaction of the United States to the Vietnam war. The camera gave us a vivid awareness of the costs of war. It gave us no inkling of the benefits — real or putative, actual or potential — of war. I do not put this down to the bias of the television reporters, though I do not exclude the possibility that some of them may have been eager to emphasise the costs. Rather, I attribute it to the nature of the television medium and, underlying that, the nature of the benefits of war. They are simply not a part of the visible reality of war; they are not tele-visible. I have racked my brain for some notion as to how a TV reporter, conscientiously intent upon giving equal coverage to benefits and to costs, could have used his camera to provide the watching public with a vivid awareness of the benefits of the American engagement in Vietnam — to no avail. I doubt that it could have been done. The easy response, the smug assertion that there were no benefits, that the American war in Vietnam was sheer wasteful, unnecessary, unrequired cost, is unworthy of serious students. We do not know what the benefits of that war were, but neither do we know that there were no benefits. In the nature of the case, TV impressed the costs upon our consciousness without helping us to develop a corresponding sense of what the war might have been intended to achieve or might, indeed, have been achieving. It showed us *that* soldiers — and others — died, and *how* they died; it could not show us *why* they died, or what might have happened if they had not died, or what might result from their dying. It may, for that reason, have contributed negatively to our understanding of the Vietnam war, and of war in general. It certainly contributed to the development of the antiwar orthodoxy which purports to insist that the credit side of any war's ledger can be nothing but a blank page.

In the perspective afforded by increased distance, temporal or spatial, the imbalance in the visibility of war's costs and benefits tends to be reversed. The price paid for war 'then and there' is not felt so keenly as a price paid 'here and now'. I shall focus my attention upon the effects of the passage of time, though much of the analysis applied also to geographical remoteness.

When a conflict becomes part of history, its costs take on an abstract quality and its results emerge to capture our attention. Rubble is cleared, buildings are replaced, and grass grows over the graves of the fallen. The Civil War battlefields of Virginia, now park-like in their beauty, are favourite haunts of tourists; people go there to picnic or to pursue the hobby of the Civil War 'buff', not to meditate on the awful price of internecine conflict. Human beings have selective memories − or perhaps we should say that memories of pain and pleasure fade at different rates. Old men idealise their childhood experiences and veterans of military service regale all who will listen with tales of fun and glory, not with stories of fear and mud and gore. The same tendency operates to reduce the conspicuousness in our collective memory of the horrors of particular wars.

That reduction permits the sense of achievement to come to the fore. But the change of attitude toward a war that has receded into the distance is not entirely a matter of our beginning to see benefits that had previously been obscured by massive costs. It is also attributable to the postwar development of consequences traceable to the war, results that could not have been visible but were at best predictable while it was running its course. Not all of these deserve entry on the credit side of the ledger, of course, but many of them may. Waging a war is rather like planting an oak tree; it may be regarded as a contribution to the welfare of future generations. One might argue that television, in its literal translation rather than in its technological meaning, *is* suitable for showing the benefits of war; while the TV camera can show only the costs, looking from a distance may enable us to see benefits that the nearsighted camera could not reveal. Whatever war can and does accomplish is likely to become a part of visible reality only after the fighting has been completed.

The revised balance sheet, drawn up in retrospect, is not necessarily a more favourable one. We are all familiar with revisionist history that represents a shift in the opposite direction, and it is true that belated entries in the ledger of a war may legitimately strengthen the conviction that it was unprofitable. On the whole, however, wars tend to look better in historical perspective. We become aware of their meaning and significance and less acutely conscious of the devastation that usually seems so senseless and pointless when one is in the middle of it.

I am reminded of a mountain that I once climbed in Pennsylvania. From a distance, its clean, sharp lines and its clear blue-green colour contribute to the pleasing quality of a tidy landscape. Hiking on its slopes, I discovered that it is anything but the neat bulk that it appears from afar. It is sheer chaos and confusion, a jumble of fallen trees, tangled vines, scattered boulders and — alas! — beer cans and twisted metal from discarded automobiles. What is the truth about the mountain? Is it a thing of ordered beauty or merely one of nature's and man's rubbish heaps? The answer depends upon where one stands.

What is the truth about a war? Do we understand it better when, in closeup view, we can see nothing but senseless violence — or when, from afar, we tend to forget its terrible toll and begin to be aware of how it fits into the historical landscape? Which is the greater handicap — the incapacity of the present to see what a war may accomplish or the incapacity of the future to remember what that war cost the people who were caught up in it?

I cannot answer those questions. They were posed for me by a student, soon after the withdrawal of American forces from Vietnam, who was disturbed because he believed that people were already forgetting how terrible that conflict had been. Would they, he asked, soon convert our Vietnam involvement into a worthy episode, an honourable segment of the nation's history? Would the truth about Vietnam be lost as myth making set in? I could answer only by raising more questions. Do we *know* that we know the whole truth, the final truth, about Vietnam? Are we certain that we, preoccupied with its costs, have a more accurate understanding of its significance for the future of mankind than will be achievable in years to come by analysts who, freed from that preoccupation, will examine it in a more dispassionate mood? Will the quality of balance in their appraisal be improved, or damaged, by the fading of the awareness of its costs that the passage of time will inevitably produce? Will the subsequent propensity for myth making distort reality more severely than our current ideological passions do?

Can we, as scholars, hope to make our retrospective evaluations of wars more, rather than less, perceptive of the truth than our contemporary judgements? To that end, we must try not to forget too much, as the present fades into the past. Equally, we must try to see as clearly as possible that which emerges from the chaos surrounding us, as the future overtakes the present.

References

1. *The History of the Peloponnesian War,* edited by Sir R.W. Livingstone *(London: Oxford University Press, 1943), Book IV, para. 59, p. 223*
2. Speech to the Manhattan Club, New York, 4 November 1915. Text in R.S. Baker and W.E. Dodd, eds., *The Public Papers of Woodrow Wilson: The New Democracy* (London and New York: Harper and Brothers, 1927), Vol. I, p. 386.
3. 'War as an Instrument of Policy' in Herbert Butterfield and Martin Wight, eds., *Diplomatic Investigations* (Cambridge, Mass: Harvard University Press, 1966), p. 199
4. *The History of the Peloponnesian War,* Book II, para. 61, p. 125

Notes on Contributors

Inis L. Claude, JR. is Edward J. Stettinius, Jr. Professor of Government and Foreign Affairs at the University of Virginia, Charlottesville; Author of *Power and International Relations*, 1962; *The Changing United Nations*, 1967; *Swords into Ploughshares*, 1971 (4th edition).

Ernst B. Haas is Professor of Political Science, Centre for International Studies, University of California, Berkeley; Author of *Beyond the Nation-State*, 1964; *The Uniting of Europe*, 1968 (2nd edition); *Tangle of Hopes; American Commitments and World Order*, 1969.

George Modelski is Professor of Political Science at the University of Washington, Seattle; Author of *A Theory of Foreign Policy*, 1962; *Principles of World Politics*, 1972.

Joseph S. Nye, JR. is Professor of Government, Centre for International Affairs at Harvard University; Author of *Pan Africanism and East African Integration*, 1965; *Peace in Parts: Integration and Conflict in Regional Organisation*, 1971; *Transnational Relations and World Politics*, 1971. (with R.O. Keohane).

Richard N. Rosecrance is Professor of International and Comparative Politics at Cornell University; Author of *Action and Reaction in World Politics*, 1963; *Defence of the Realm: Strategy in the Nuclear Epoch*, 1968; *International Relations: Peace or War?*, 1973.

Bruce M. Russett is Professor of Political Science, Yale; Joint Author of *World Handbook of Political and Social Indicators, et al.*, 1964; Author of *Military Forces and American Society*, 1973, (with (ed.) A.C. Stephan); (ed.) *Economic Theories of World Politics*, 1968.

Geoffrey L. Goodwin is Montague Burton Professor of International Relations, London School of Economics and Political Science.

Andrew Linklater is Noel Buxton Student in International Relations, London School of Economics and Political Science.